Album of Spaceflight

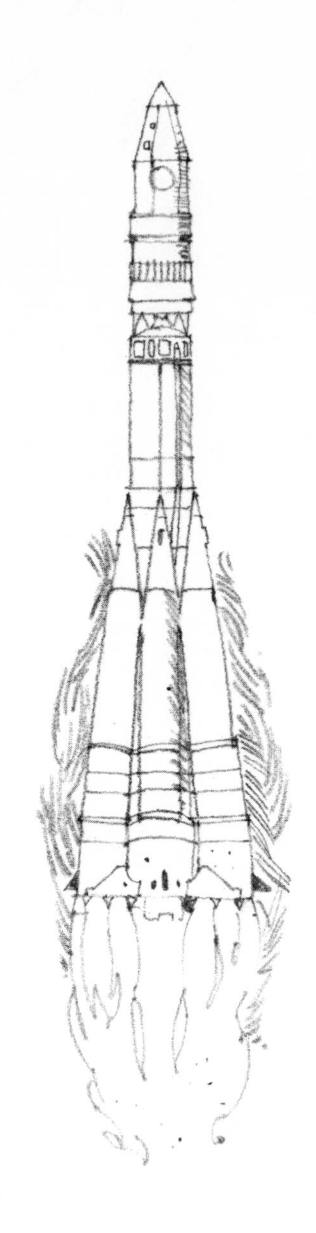

ALBUM OF SPACEFLIGHT

THIS EXCITING and well-researched volume traces the most important moments in the history of spaceflight, from the earliest attempts to reach outer space to the amazing future of the space frontier.

Author Tom McGowen begins with the compelling story of the first rockets, the early satellites and unmanned flights, and the successes and disappointments of the first manned flights. Later chapters detail the race for the Moon, explorations of the farthest planets, and exciting new technologies like Skylab and the space shuttle. A final chapter tells what lies ahead for the development of space—be it space stations, huge telecommunications structures, mining operations, military satellites, power stations, or space events now barely imagined.

Throughout, the author shows the contributions of both the American and Soviet space programs for a clear picture of the chronology and impact of each. A calendar of spaceflights and an index at the back of the book are featured as additional aids to the reader.

Lee Brubaker's talented brush brings the story of spaceflight vividly to life. Thirteen full-color pages and over 50 black and white illustrations depict particularly dramatic and informative aspects of spaceflight. Each illustration is as carefully researched and documented as the fascinating text. ALBUM OF SPACEFLIGHT has been newly updated and demonstrates the readability, scientific accuracy, and timeliness that make the books in the ALBUM series so valuable.

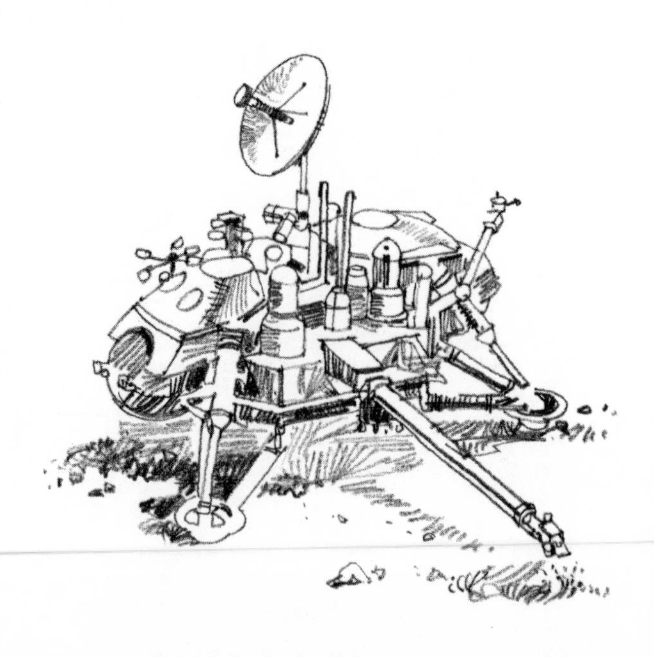

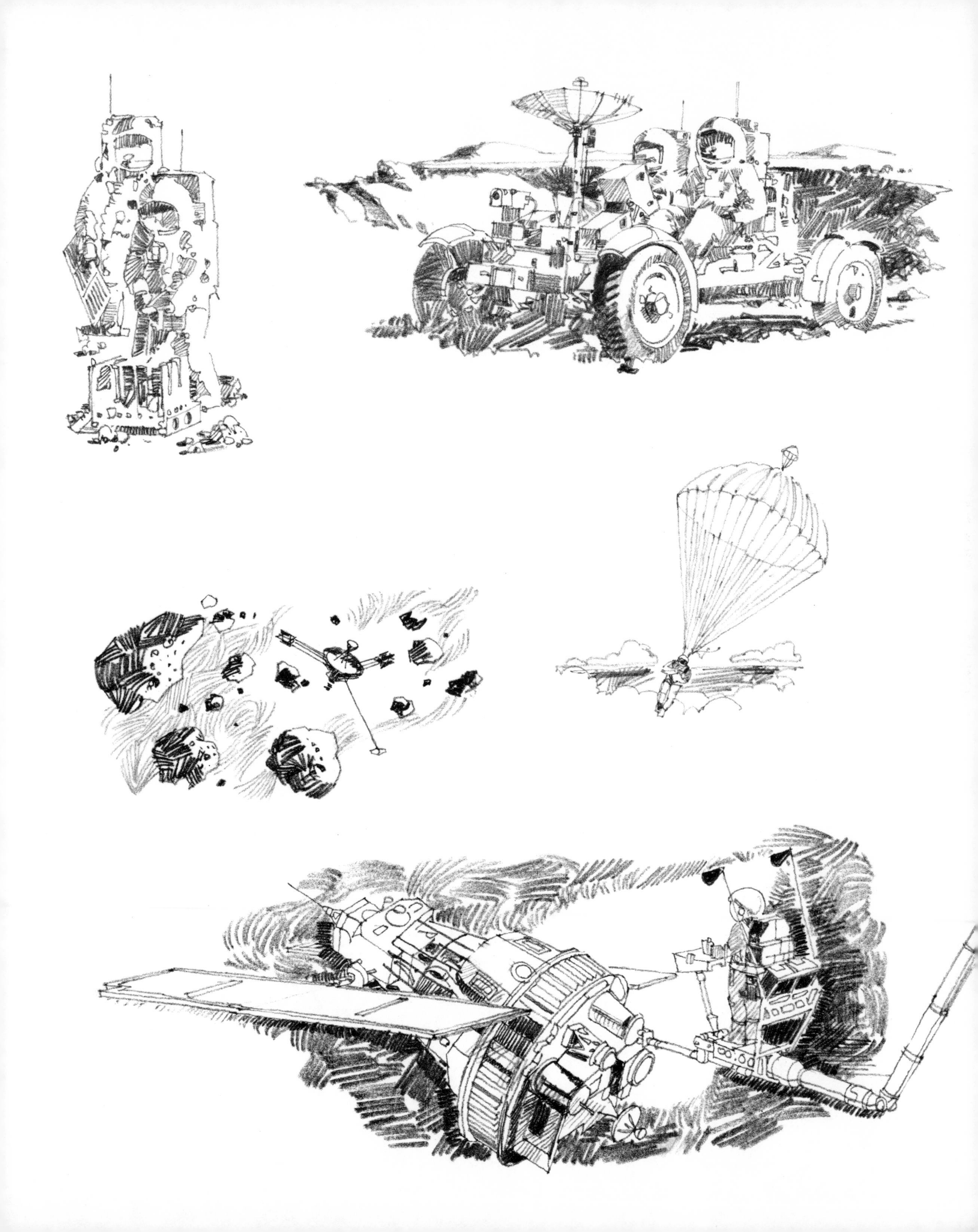

Album of Spaceflight

Revised and Updated Edition

By TOM McGOWEN
Illustrated by LEE BRUBAKER

CHECKERBOARD PRESS
New York

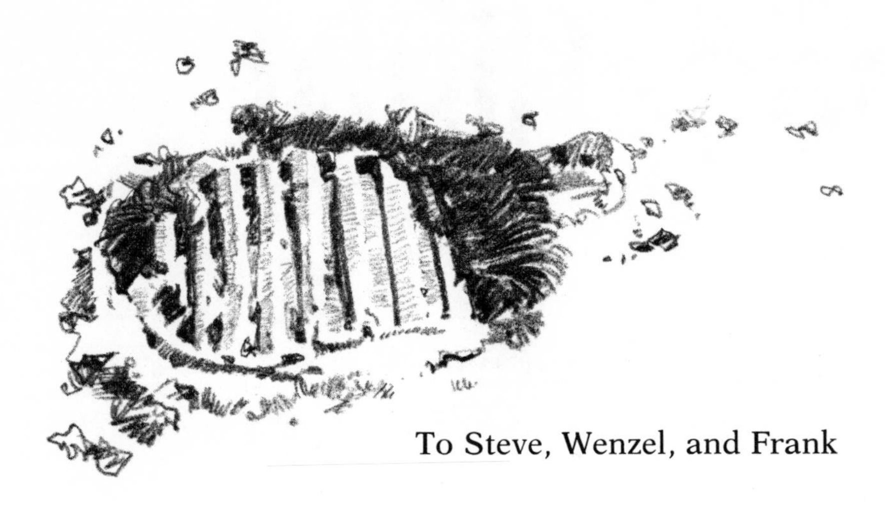

To Steve, Wenzel, and Frank

Text and illustrations reviewed and authenticated by Dr. James Sweitzer, Astronomer, Chicago, Illinois

Library of Congress Cataloging-in-Publication Data
McGowen, Tom.
Album of spaceflight.
Reprint. Originally published: © 1983.
Includes index.
Summary: Discusses the history of space flight from the first rockets and satellites to a projection of a future with power plants in space and people living on space stations.
1. Space flight—Juvenile literature. [1. Space flight] I. Brubaker, Lee, ill. II. Sweitzer, James. III. Title.
TL793.M39 1987 629.4 86-31759
ISBN 0-02-688509-3 (hardcover)
ISBN 0-02-688502-6 (softcover)

Contents

Solving the Problems of Spaceflight

SINCE THE YEAR 1961, more than 100 people have gone into space; men have explored the Moon; robot spacecraft have been sent to explore all but one of the Solar System's planets. You are living in the age of space. But less than 40 years ago, most people thought of spaceships and voyages to other planets as silly dreams that could never come true. Less than 5 years before the first human went into space and returned, most people would have laughed at anyone who said such a thing could be done!

Spaceflight seemed impossible because there were enormous problems to be solved before it could be accomplished. One problem was simply power. Just to get out into the beginning of space—the point at which Earth's atmosphere, or air, ends—an object has to be able to escape the clutch of Earth's gravity, which seeks to pull everything down to Earth's surface. The object has to be able to push upward harder than gravity pulls downward. This requires enormous power, and up until about 30 years ago, there was no kind of engine that could produce anything near the amount of power needed for such a push.

Another problem was, how could a spacecraft maneuver, or turn and change direction, in space? An airplane turns by means of flaps on its wings and tail; the push of air on those flaps swings the plane in different directions. But there is no air in space, so flaps or rudders would be useless on a spacecraft. It seemed as if once a spacecraft was in space, moving in a particular direction, it would have to keep moving in that same direction forever! How could it be made to change course?

Aside from the problems of getting a vehicle into space and then making it go where you wanted, there were a good many questions concerning the people who would be aboard such a vehicle. Could humans stand the tremendous acceleration, or buildup of speed, it would

APOLLO 12 FLIGHT
TO THE MOON

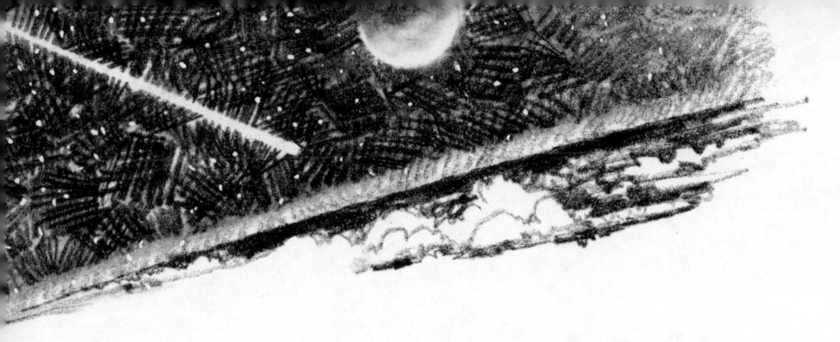

take to push a craft into space? Or would such acceleration—many times the pull of gravity—tear a human body apart, as many people believed? And if humans could stand the stress of getting into space, would they then be able to stand the lack of gravity? It is the pull of gravity that gives all things their weight. But out in orbit, falling free in space, things would have absolutely no weight and would float! Could a human body take that? Would the blood in a human body continue to flow without gravity? Would the lungs be able to keep working? Many people thought not.

Then there was also what scientists called the reentry problem: How could a spacecraft be kept from turning into a meteor when it returned to Earth from space? A meteor, or shooting star, is a chunk of rock that comes hurtling into Earth's atmosphere and burns up. It burns because of friction—the rubbing of the rock against the air at such speed causes tremendous heat. How could a spacecraft be kept from burning up like a meteor as it rushed down through the atmosphere at thousands of miles an hour?

The problems of spaceflight did, indeed, seem overwhelming. But, one by one, a little at a time, they were solved.

Just before the beginning of the twentieth century, a shy, bespectacled, middle-aged Russian schoolteacher named Konstantin Tsiolkovsky figured out the kind of engine needed to power a spacecraft—a rocket engine. A rocket, of the sort used in fireworks displays, pushes up into the sky because energy is pushing down out of its tail in a gush of fire. A push in one direction causes an equal push in the opposite direction. Tsiolkovsky worked out the mathematics to show that a big enough rocket with enough fuel could push itself right off Earth. He also determined that a burst of energy from a rocket engine on one side of a craft in space would push the craft in the opposite direction. Thus, rocket engines were the answer to maneuvering a spacecraft in the airless void, as well as the answer to getting them there.

In the early 1900's, an American college teacher, Dr. Robert Goddard, began doing experiments with rockets. He tested them with different kinds of fuels to see how fast and how high he could make them go. He tested them inside compartments from which all the air had been pumped to see if they would work in airless space—and proved they worked very well.

In 1923, Hermann Oberth, a Rumanian student in Germany, published a small book that showed how a spaceship might be built, launched, and guided on a journey from Earth to other planets. Some of the ideas in the book really belonged to Tsiolkovsky and Goddard, but Oberth had come up with some new, good ideas of his own. These three men—Tsiolkovsky, Goddard, and Oberth—were the pioneers of the science of spaceflight. They solved some of the hardest problems.

During the 1930's, big steps were taken toward spaceflight—in secret. The Ger-

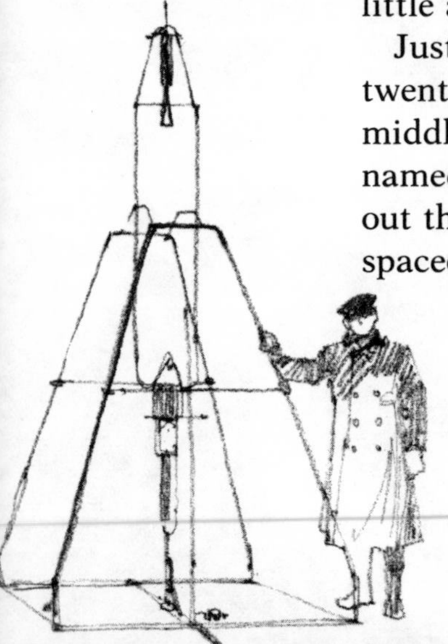

Dr. Goddard and his
Liquid-Fuel Rocket

man army began trying to build rockets that could travel through the air for hundreds of miles at high speed. These rockets weren't to be used for spaceflight, however; they were to be weapons—giant flying bombs! But many of the problems that had to be solved in order to build a spacecraft would have to be solved in order to build these war rockets. And many of the problems were solved by using the ideas of Tsiolkovsky, Goddard, and Oberth.

During World War II, rocket bombs called V-2's caused death and destruction. Launched in Germany, they would travel hundreds of miles to come down and explode in Belgium or England. Looking like a huge torpedo standing on four big fins, a V-2 held a large quantity of liquid oxygen and alcohol in its fuel tanks. When this fuel was set on fire in the ignition, or burning, chamber at the base of the rocket, it created a continuous explosion of energy. The energy poured, with a tremendous thrust, out of the rocket's bottom. This thrust slowly lifted the huge, heavy object off the ground. The constant thrust made the rocket move faster and higher. It went rushing off into the sky in a great curve, reaching a speed of about 3,500 miles an hour. Even when the last of its fuel was used up, the V-2's momentum, the force with which it moved, kept it going until it reached the highest point of its curved path, or trajectory. It then began to fall back toward Earth. But at that highest point of its trajectory—an altitude of 60 miles—it was almost in space! All the scientists who worked on these bombs knew that what they had built was nearly a spacecraft!

After the war, many V-2's and people who had worked on them went to the United States or the Soviet Union. Both of these nations began experimenting with V-2's and building similar rockets of their own. Many V-2's were adapted to become launch vehicles—vessels that could carry smaller craft up almost into space. Then the smaller craft's own rocket engines would be ignited to push the smaller craft still higher. When two craft are used in this way, the launch vehicle is known as the first stage, the vehicle it "boosts" up toward space is called the second stage.

By this method, both the United States and the Soviet Union began sending vessels higher and higher. More and more was learned. Fuels were improved. Ever better launch vehicles and second-stage craft were built.

During the late 1940's and early 1950's, the problems of spaceflight were steadily being solved.

The goal of both the United States and the Soviet Union was to send an object far enough and fast enough into space so that Earth's gravity would only be able to hold on to it, not quite pull it back. Then the object would be in orbit, circling around and around Earth like an artificial moon. When this could be done, the age of space would begin!

V-2 Rocket Bomb

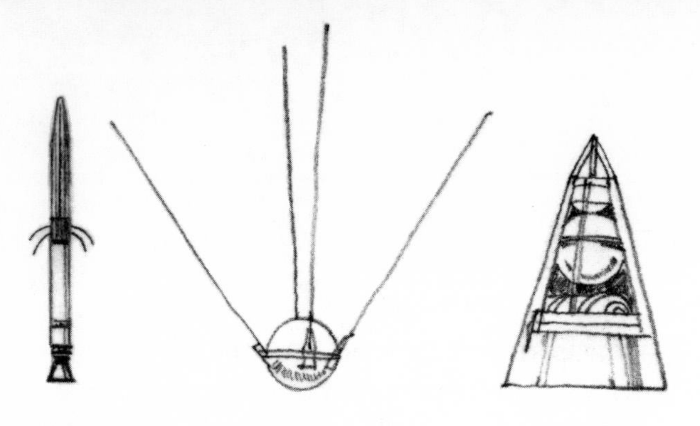

Explorer 1, Sputnik 1, Sputnik 2—Relative Sizes

The Beginning of the Space Age

THE UNENDING BLACKNESS of space spreads in all directions from the edge of the blue haze of atmosphere that surrounds our planet, Earth. Within that blackness hang the countless billions of tiny lights that are the stars. Outside Earth's atmosphere, the stars appear as unwinking glows, for it is the restless movement of our air that makes stars seem to twinkle. And from the edge of Earth's atmosphere, the stars appear to hang motionless, for it is only the slow spin of our planet itself that makes them appear to creep at a snail's pace across the sky when they are watched from the ground. In space, those tiny points of light do not move.

But on a day in October, in the year 1957, had someone been able to peer out into space from a certain point high above Earth, that person might have seen one single tiny speck of light, among all the glowing specks, that *was* moving. This light would have appeared to be rushing rapidly through the darkness in a great curving path that followed the curve of the huge globe of Earth below. But this moving gleam was an alien, artificial thing, no "native" of space! It was a basketball-sized globe of metal, from which sprouted four slim metal rods. Human beings of Earth had put an object into space. A tiny metal moon, its mirror-bright surface gleaming with reflected sunlight, was moving in orbit, around and around the planet. It was a breathtaking, awesome event in human history!

This artificial satellite had been launched by the government of the Soviet Union and was called *Sputnik,* a Russian word meaning "satellite." The 23-inch-wide, 184-pound hollow metal ball had been fastened inside the pointed nose or cone of a giant rocket that was sent thundering up from Earth into the edge of space. At a height of 142 miles and a speed of nearly 5 miles a second, the nose cone was automatically hurled out of the way, and the metal ball was separated from the rocket. Continuing to move at the same speed but prevented by Earth's gravity from moving in a straight line out into space, the ball went into orbit around the planet—like a ball attached to a rubber band held in a person's hand and swung around and around in an ellipse. For the next three months, Sputnik made a complete orbit, or circle, around the Earth

SPUTNIK 1 SEPARATES
FROM ITS ROCKET

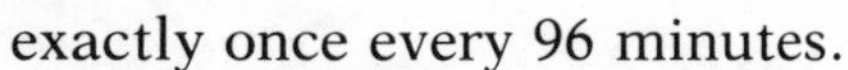
Inside Sputnik 1

exactly once every 96 minutes.

When news of Sputnik's successful launch was released, the world was overwhelmed with excitement. In the United States, the excitement was mixed with disappointment, for the Americans were very close to putting a satellite of their own into space and had hoped to be first. But still, all over America as all over the world, people looked up at the sky, thrilled to be alive at the time of such a tremendous happening!

However, although getting Sputnik into orbit had been a tremendous accomplishment, it wasn't the end of the job. The Soviet scientists and technicians wanted Sputnik to answer some questions for them. For example, if humans were ever to go into space, the inside of a spacecraft would have to be kept at a steady, comfortable temperature for them. The people who had put Sputnik into space wanted to be sure that their method of keeping its inside temperature steady and comfortable was working. So the inside of the hollow metal ball contained instruments that could send back to Earth, by means of radio signals, information on temperature and other things. Thus, from the lifeless metal ball rushing along its circular path around the world came information that would be of great use in preparing for future journeys into space.

And the next spaceflight wasn't long in coming. On November 3 of 1957, just about a month after Sputnik had been launched and while people everywhere were still marveling over it, the Soviets launched a second spacecraft. This one was also called Sputnik—Sputnik 2—but it was quite different from Sputnik 1. It was a 12-foot-long cone, and it weighed almost 1,000 pounds more than the little metal ball. It had to be bigger and heavier than Sputnik 1 because, as the world was astonished and delighted to hear, it carried a passenger! Strapped into a comfortable, thickly padded couch was the first Earth creature to go into orbit in space—a female dog named Laika!

The scientists of the Soviet Union had decided that before a person could be sent into space, it would be necessary to find out what effect the acceleration, weightlessness, and other conditions of spaceflight would have on a human. They could only find out by sending a large, living, intelligent creature whose body worked in the same way as a human body, and so they chose to send a dog. Laika had been put through a training program just as if she were a human pilot. She had been taught not to be frightened by the noise, shaking, and pressure of a rocket takeoff. The chamber of the spacecraft in which she rode was padded, air-conditioned, and heated to keep her as comfortable as possible. It also contained machinery to automatically serve her portions of food at regular periods of time. Instruments kept record of her heartbeat, breathing, and other bodily activities and sent the information back to Earth by radio. The instruments showed that Laika was calm and unafraid during her seven days in orbit—a true heroine!

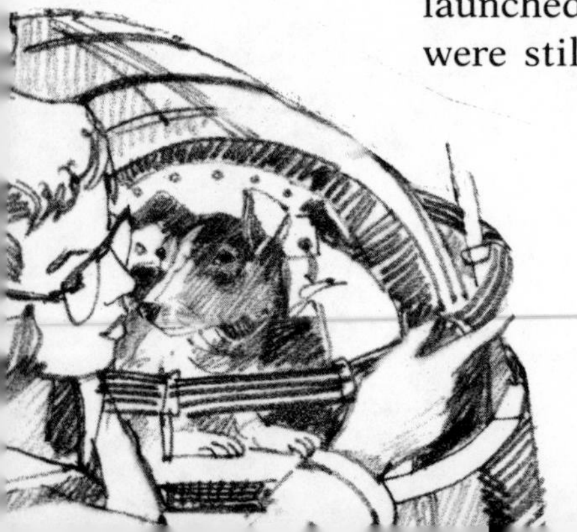
Laika is strapped into Sputnik 2.

Of course, everyone knew there was no way to bring the brave dog safely down; for at that time, there was no way to bring a spacecraft back automatically. After seven days, Sputnik 2 would drop so low that it would be back in Earth's atmosphere and would soon burn up from friction. But the people who had put Laika into space had seen to it that she wouldn't suffer—the last portion of her food contained a painless, quick-acting poison. After eating her food, Laika just went to sleep and never woke up. But her week in orbit had helped prove that human beings could survive in space!

At 9:42 on the night of January 31, 1958, a little less than three months after Laika had been put into orbit, the United States put its first artificial satellite into space. At Cape Canaveral, Florida, a thundering cloud of smoke and sand belched out from beneath a huge, gleaming white U.S. Army Juno I rocket. The rocket lifted off the ground and soared upward into the night sky, carrying the satellite known as Explorer 1 into orbit.

Explorer 1 looked like a stovepipe. It was a metal tube 6 inches wide, about 6½ feet long, and weighing only some 30 pounds. But it went into a higher orbit than either Sputnik, and its instruments made a startling—and rather frightening—discovery. They revealed that at a height above 600 miles there was apparently a "belt" of deadly radiation around Earth, radiation that might cause the death of any human who went through it! For a time, it was feared this meant that humans would never be able to go any farther into space, that we could never do more than make close-in orbits around our planet. But other American satellites, sent up later, showed that space vehicles could be protected by means of metal shielding.

Thus, from October 4, 1957, to January 31, 1958, a period of only four months, two of Earth's major nations had put artificial satellites into space and had made important new discoveries. The exploration of space was now definitely underway, and the age of space had truly begun!

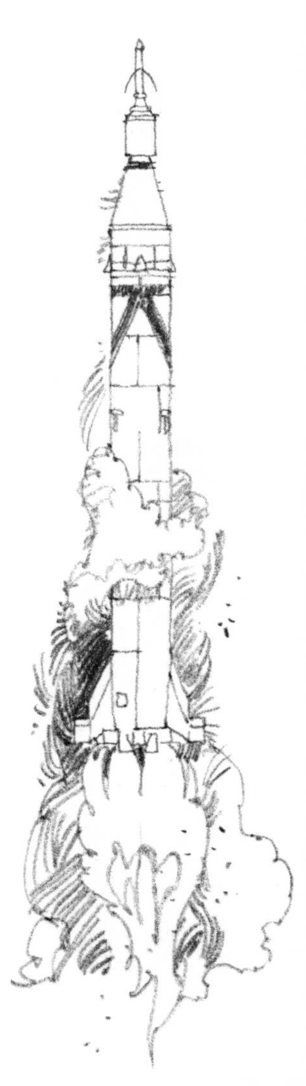

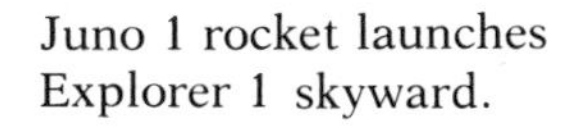

Juno 1 rocket launches Explorer 1 skyward.

The First Human in Space

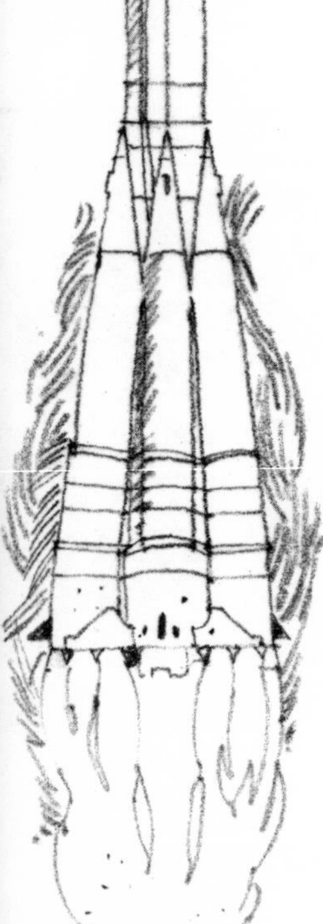

Vostok 1
Launch Vehicle

ON THE TWELFTH OF APRIL in the year 1961, a young Russian man by the name of Yuri Alexeyevich Gagarin lay on a thickly padded chairlike couch inside a hollow metal ball crammed with instruments and machinery. The ball, in turn, was inside the hollow conical tip of a giant rocket that towered among a cluster of buildings and scaffolding in a flat desert valley in southeastern Russia. Gagarin's eyes looked through a broad glass plate in a round helmet that fitted over his entire head, and his body was swathed in a bulky, one-piece garment designed to enable him to survive intense heat, intense cold, or total airlessness. He was a pilot in his nation's air force and a skilled flier. But today he was to make a flight such as no one had ever made before—the first flight of a human into space.

The metal ball in which Gagarin lay was known as a command module. It was airtight, air-conditioned, and heated to a steady, comfortable temperature. It was attached to a squat, conical base called an instrument compartment, which contained a single rocket engine. The command module and instrument compartment together formed a spacecraft which was named *Vostok,* meaning "East."

The rocket that would carry Vostok and Gagarin into space was what is known as a multistage rocket. Vostok sat atop the final stage of this rocket, a metal cylinder containing a rocket engine, which in turn sat atop the core stage, around which were grouped several booster-stage rocket engines. All together, the core stage and booster stage contained 20 rocket engines that would lift the entire huge, tapering assembly off Earth.

All was ready. In a nearby building, people bent anxiously over instruments. A voice monotonously counted off seconds: "—six—five—four—three—two—one—"

Flame blossomed around the bottom of the towering rocket. A steady, thunderous roar shook the plain. Energy poured down out of the 20 huge engines that formed the base of the rocket, straining with titanic force against the grip of gravity. The rocket shuddered as slowly, *slowly* that tremendous thrust lifted it off the ground.

It seemed to pause for a moment, balancing on the smoke and flame pouring out of the bottom. Then because of the

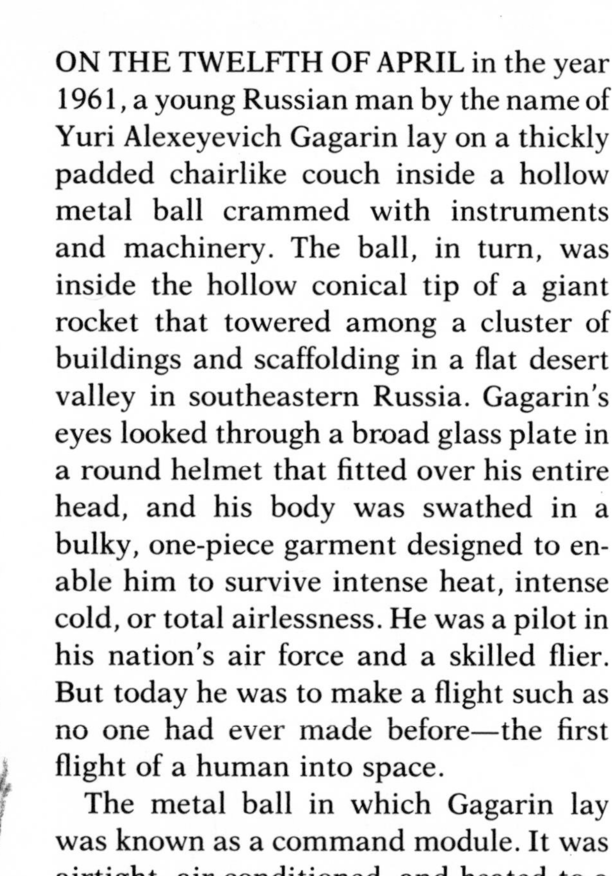

COSMONAUT GAGARIN
INSIDE VOSTOK 1

CC

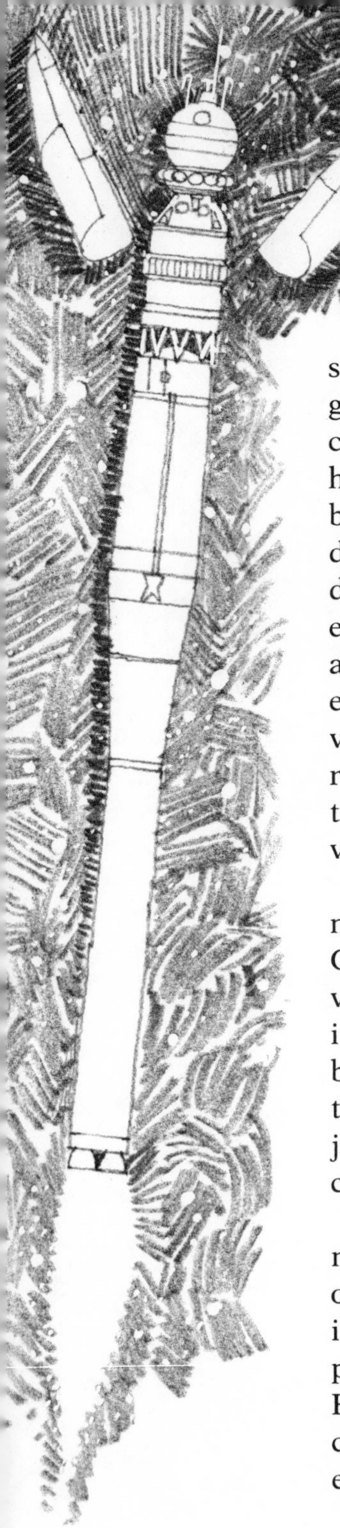

Nose cone pops off the command module.

steady thrust of its engines, the rocket began to rise, gathering speed. Inside the command module, Gagarin felt as if a heavy weight were lying upon his entire body, grinding him down against the padding of the chair-couch. This was the force due to inertia, the same force that pushes each occupant of an automobile back against the seat as the car begins to accelerate. But in Gagarin's case, that push was being multiplied many times as the rocket, accelerating tremendously, sought to free itself from the clutch of gravity that would pull it back to Earth.

Despite this crushing pressure, the noise, and the shuddering of his vessel, Gagarin felt fine. Most people's hearts would have been racing with excitement in such a situation. But Gagarin's pulse, being measured by an instrument back at the launching site, was only around 75—just about normal for someone sitting in a chair on Earth, reading a book!

The nose cone covering the command-module ball had automatically popped off, and through one of the small portholes in his round craft, Gagarin could see a portion of Russia spread out below him. He spoke into the radiotelephone that connected him to Earth. "I see land covered with haze. I feel well."

The shuddering and the noise had stopped. The final rocket stage had done its job and carried Gagarin into space. Its fuel was now used up, and it automatically separated from the command module and instrument compartment, which continued by themselves. They were now so high that Gagarin could see, through the porthole, the vast, curving edge of the huge ball that is the planet Earth. Looking at the broad curve of Earth's horizon spread out before him, Gagarin saw that our world's atmosphere, or covering of air, formed a lovely bluish halo surrounding the planet. At the bottom of this misty ring of color was a broad band of sky-blue, which gave way to dark blue, then violet as the air got thinner. Above the violet stretched the solid black "sky" of outer space. It seemed to Gagarin that the stars glittering in that utter blackness were much brighter and sharper than when seen from Earth.

Vostok was now in orbit; it had become a tiny satellite, moving in a vast circle around Earth. It was traveling at a speed of many thousands of miles an hour, but there was no longer any pressure, and Gagarin was as comfortable as he might have been sitting in his home on Earth. For he was moving with the spacecraft, just as we are moving with the "spacecraft" Earth—which is rushing through space at many thousands of miles an hour.

There was no longer any gravity at work in Vostok. Gagarin was feeling the strange sensation of being light enough to float, for he was actually floating, in a seated position, in the air above his chair. It was an odd feeling, but he soon grew used to it. It seemed easier to do things without gravity, he found. However, there were problems—as he was writing in a notebook, he had to hold the notebook down so

Gagarin sees Earth
through Vostok's porthole.

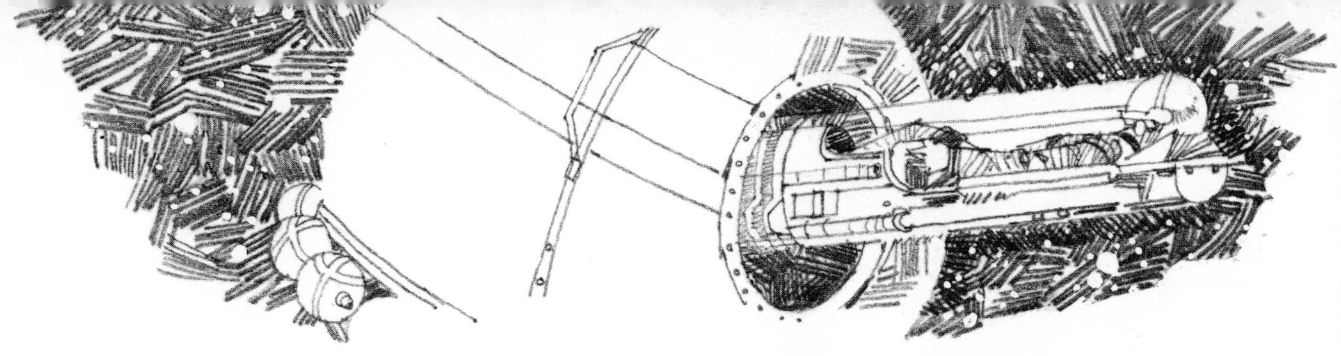

it wouldn't float away from him!

Gagarin was to make one complete orbit of Earth and then bring Vostok down near where it had been launched. During the time in orbit, there were a good many tasks to be done, and the *cosmonaut,* or "space sailor," busied himself as the craft sped on its way. Shortly before 10:00 A.M., Moscow time, less than an hour after the launching, Vostok was more than halfway around the world, over South America. Gagarin radioed that the flight was proceeding normally and that he felt well. By 10:15, he was over Africa. There were only 40 minutes left to go.

They passed swiftly. Vostok was nearly over the point from which it had been launched. At the proper moment, the technicians on Earth instructed Gagarin, by radio, to land. At once, he switched on an instrument that lined the ship up properly. He then fired the single rocket engine that was part of the instrument compartment.

A blast of energy poured forth in the direction in which the vessel was moving. This served as a brake, slowing the spacecraft's speed. When the flare of flame died out, the whole instrument compartment separated from the command module in which Gagarin sat. He was now in a wingless, powerless, heavy metal ball that was falling toward Earth at a speed of some 300 feet a second—just about 1 mile every quarter of a minute! Only a special shell around the outside of the ball kept it from burning up from friction as it cut through the air at that speed.

At a little more than 4 miles above the ground, a hatch opened in the side of the ball. Two seconds later, the padded chair in which Gagarin was strapped was hurled through the opening, out of the spacecraft. At once, a large parachute attached to Gagarin's space suit billowed open. The first man to go into space floated gently to Earth. He landed safely, minutes later, near a Russian village.

The command module continued to plummet toward Earth. But at about 2½ miles above the ground, a huge parachute automatically opened, and Vostok, too, dropped gently to Earth and landed undamaged. One of the greatest achievements in human history had come to a safe and successful end.

Until Yuri Gagarin became the first human to go into space and return, a great many people still doubted that space travel was possible for humans. They feared that a human couldn't stand the terrible pressure of the launching from Earth or that a human body couldn't work right without gravity. Gagarin's magnificent adventure proved that space travel was safe.

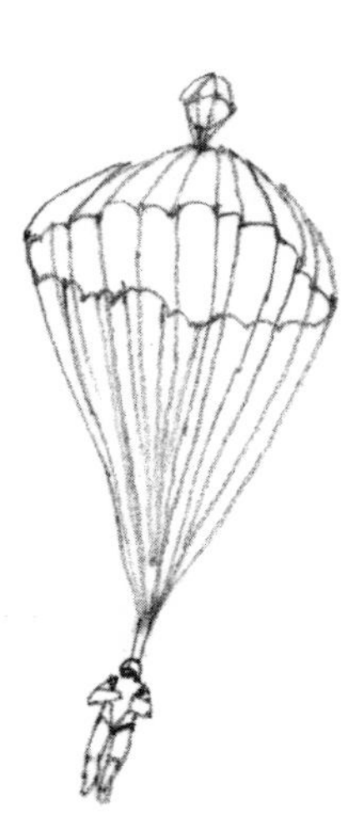

Gagarin ejects and floats to Earth.

Voskhod 2—the First Space Walk

The "Space Walks"

WITHIN LESS THAN A YEAR after Gagarin's historic flight, other brave men had been launched into space and returned safely. Gherman Titov, another Russian cosmonaut, orbited Earth. Americans Alan Shepard and Virgil "Gus" Grissom made flights, without going into orbit, as part of the first U.S. manned program, Project Mercury. And John Glenn, in Mercury 6, became the first U.S. astronaut to orbit Earth. As time passed, more men and one woman made Earth orbits. The age of space was well underway!

But in both the United States and the Soviet Union, scientists wondered and worried over a problem. All the people who had gone into space had, of course, been inside vessels. But everyone knew that if human beings were truly going to conquer space, they would have to be able, at times, to go outside of a ship in space. There would be situations when the outside of a spacecraft would need repairs or when the crew of one vessel might have to move to another vessel while both were in space. Also, scientists had hopes of someday building space stations in orbit, and to do that, people would have to be able to move about and work in space, protected only by space suits. But would people be able to do such a thing? Could a human being *stand* to float in space, many hundreds of miles above Earth, without having the protective walls of a spaceship around him or her?

In 1965, both the United States and the Soviet Union conducted experiments to see how a human could handle a "walk" in space. On March 18, after many months of preparation and training, the Russians sent two men, Pavel Ivanovich Belyayev and Alexei Arkhipovich Leonov, into orbit aboard a spacecraft called Voskhod 2. Belyayev was the ship's pilot, and Leonov was to be the first human to go outside a ship in space. He was equipped with a new type of space suit that enabled him to move easily. The suit would also protect him from the intense heat and dazzling glare of sunlight—much hotter and brighter in airless space than on Earth, where it is scattered and filtered by miles and miles of thick atmosphere. A telephone was built into Leonov's helmet so that he could stay in constant contact with Belyayev. Belyayev wore a similar suit, just in case it might be necessary for him to go out and rescue Leonov.

LEONOV IN THE AIR LOCK
OF VOSKHOD 2

СССР

As soon as Voskhod 2 went into orbit, Leonov began his historic experiment. He pulled himself into a special small chamber called an air lock. Closing the hatch behind him, he sealed off the air lock from Voskhod's cabin. At the other side of the air lock was a round hatch, and after waiting ten minutes, Leonov opened this. Through the opening showed blackness and stars. Once Leonov went through that opening, he would be outside Voskhod, in space. A long lifeline—a tough, flexible cord attached to his space suit—was fastened inside the ship so that he couldn't float away.

Leonov put his head and shoulders out of the opening. It was much the same sort of thing as if a man in a diving suit were to stick his head out of a porthole in a submarine under the sea. But instead of having water all around him, Leonov had only the emptiness of space. Carefully, he pushed himself up and out through the hatchway. He hesitated for a moment, and then with an action that took tremendous courage, he pushed himself gently away from the ship so that he would drift out as far as the lifeline would let him. Slowly, the line stretched to its full length, finally bringing Leonov to a stop some 16 feet away from the ship. He floated at the end of the line, a tiny figure surrounded by the black immensity of outer space.

Amazing though it may seem, Leonov's slight push had actually moved the spacecraft, and he noticed that it was turning slowly. He couldn't have budged it a millimeter on Earth, but here in space it was weightless, and his gentlest touch could make it move!

Leonov was moving through space at the same speed as the ship, so he was no more conscious of moving than he had been when in the ship. But he was spinning slowly at the end of the lifeline, like a wheel on an axle. For a few moments he would find himself looking upon the vastness of space: dense blackness spangled with stars. Then, gradually, his rotation would turn him toward Earth, and he felt as if he were swimming above a gigantic map. He could recognize the Volga River, a tiny, crawling silver thread far below, and the rugged range of the Ural Mountains, like wads of crumpled paper.

This was the moment the doctors and scientists had wondered about. Could a human being stand to float in space, surrounded by endless black nothingness? Might a fear of falling hundreds of miles to Earth affect a person's mind? Would this experiment, in which Leonov was the guinea pig, show after all that human beings could not stand to be outside a ship in space?

What the experiment showed was quite the opposite. Leonov felt fine and was in good spirits. He discovered that he was enjoying himself! At the end of 10 minutes, when Belyayev notified him it was time for him to return to the ship, Leonov was having so much fun that he actually didn't want to go back inside the spacecraft!

Some ten weeks later, on June 3, the

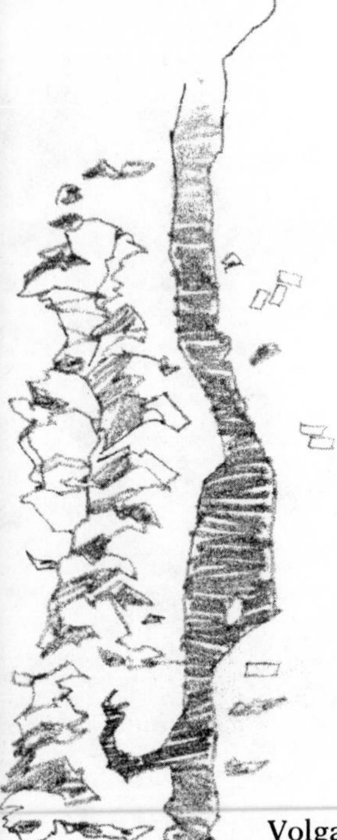

Volga River Seen From Space

American space program conducted its space-walk experiment. Astronauts James McDivitt and Edward White were launched into orbit in a spacecraft labeled Gemini 4. The space walk was to be performed by White, at the end of a 25-foot lifeline. However, unlike Leonov, who could only drift at the end of his line, White would be able to move around by means of a propulsion gun; a "rocket" gun that fired bursts of compressed, or squeezed, air. The thrust of the air as it left the propulsion gun would shove White in the opposite direction. In this way, he could move himself around the outside of the spacecraft.

Gemini 4 was about 100 miles above Earth, traveling at a speed of 17,000 miles an hour, and nearly over the island of Hawaii when White pushed himself into space. He drifted out the full length of his lifeline. Using the propulsion gun, he began to move himself about.

White found, as Leonov had, that floating in space was a very pleasant experience. "This is fun," he exclaimed at one point. When McDivitt finally told him to return to the ship, White lamented, "It's the saddest moment of my life!"

Two men had now proved that floating in open space was not the frightening experience most scientists had feared it would be. For people such as White and Leonov, at least, it was fun! This showed that in the future, men and women could work outside ships in space and would be able to control their movements with some kind of propulsion unit such as White had used. It was a giant step in the conquest of space!

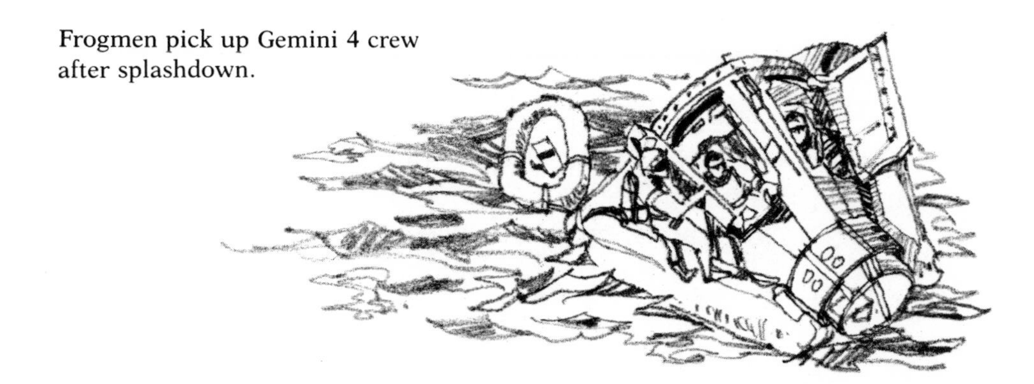

Frogmen pick up Gemini 4 crew after splashdown.

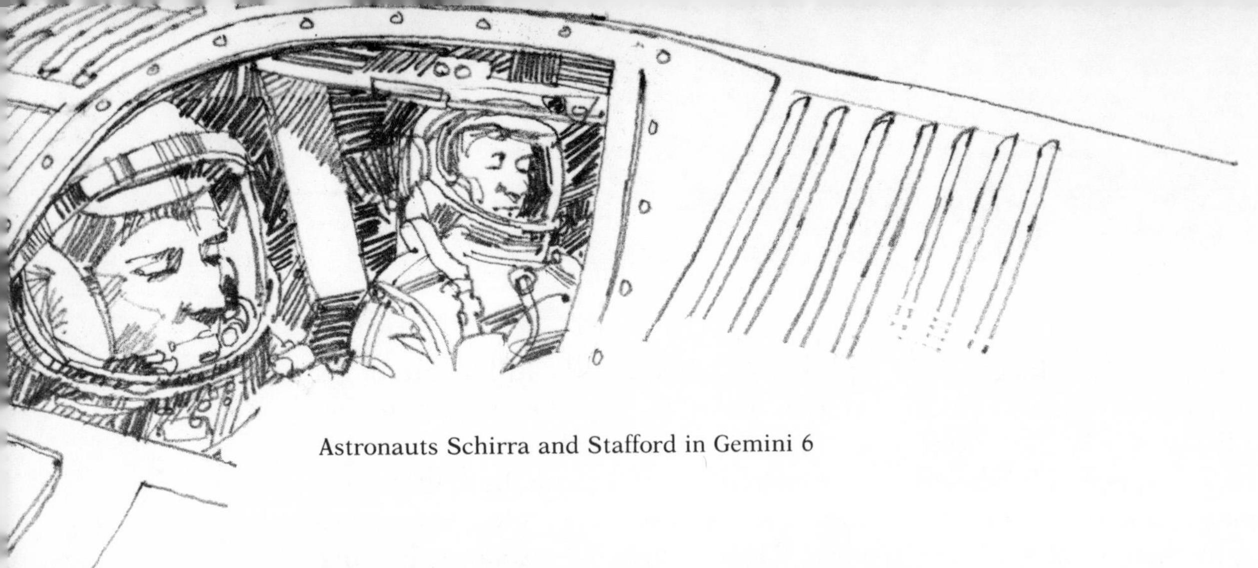

Astronauts Schirra and Stafford in Gemini 6

Linking Up in Space

IN THE BLACKNESS of space, a silvery object moved in a vast circle around the great blue-and-white ball of Earth. Far behind it, a second object gleamed in the darkness—a pair of spacecraft in orbit.

Slowly, very slowly, it seemed, the second craft was gaining on the first, closing the distance between them. Despite this seeming slowness, the craft was actually racing through the darkness at a speed of many thousands of miles an hour. So was the vessel ahead. It was the job of the man piloting the second craft to bring it close enough to touch the first. But what would happen when they touched at that speed?

Before a ship of the sea can put people or cargo onto land, it has to dock. The ship is carefully guided alongside a platform called a dock, its engines are shut off, and it is tied up with cables that fasten it to sturdy posts. The two spacecraft moving in their orbits around Earth were like a ship and a dock. They were going to answer the question of whether a ship of space could dock *in* space. Could a craft moving at hundreds of miles a minute be brought close enough to become fastened to another object moving at hundreds of miles a minute, without damage to either?

This question had to be answered. The building of a space station that would move around Earth in an unending orbit was the goal of space scientists. Such a station would be tremendously useful. But if such a station was built, people and supplies would have to be brought to it by ships sent from Earth. And those ships of space would have to dock, somehow, just as ships of the sea must.

By October 25, 1965, the American space program was ready for the first attempt to have one spacecraft dock with another. A huge Atlas first-stage rocket, carrying a smaller Agena rocket, blasted off from Cape Canaveral, Florida. When the Atlas had boosted it high enough, the Agena would separate and go into orbit. Just about 90 minutes later, a Gemini spacecraft, labeled Gemini 6 and carrying astronauts Walter Schirra and Thomas Stafford, would be launched to follow the Agena into orbit and dock with it. In the back of the Agena was an opening big enough for the Gemini's nose to slide into. This opening was fitted with a ring that

GEMINI 8 CAPSULE
APPROACHES THE AGENA

UNITED
STATES

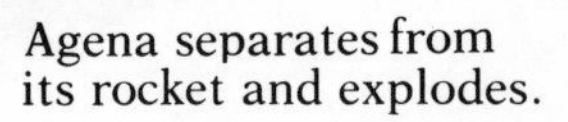
Agena separates from its rocket and explodes.

would close around Gemini 6, locking it securely into place. Astronaut Schirra, the Gemini's pilot, had trained for months to bring his ship's nose into that opening on the Agena.

But, suddenly, all that training seemed wasted! As the Agena separated from the Atlas booster, it exploded! Quickly, the order was given to stop the launching of Gemini 6. There was no point in continuing, now that there was nothing for it to dock with.

It was a bad setback, but scientists and technicians did what they could to salvage things. Gemini 6 was still ready to go, and Gemini 7 was being made ready for launching within the next few months. Neither Gemini had a dock opening as the Agena did. But it would be possible to use them to test everything up to the actual moment of docking—to test a spacecraft pilot's ability to move one vessel into docking position with another.

Gemini 7 was launched on December 4, crewed by astronauts Frank Borman and James Lovell. They would be in orbit for two weeks, longer than anyone else had ever stayed in space. There would be plenty of time to get Gemini 6 onto the launchpad and ready to go.

Gemini 6 was scheduled to be launched on December 12, when Gemini 7 would be at exactly the right point in space. But once again, Gemini 6's astronauts, Wally Schirra and Tom Stafford, were disappointed. Smoke and flame poured from the bottom of the Titan rocket that was to boost their Gemini craft into orbit, but there was no lift-off. Something had gone wrong, and the Titan engines automatically shut themselves off. The launch was canceled for that day.

Three days later, the problem had been found and solved, and the Titan went roaring skyward. Gemini 6 separated from the booster and went into orbit, seeking Gemini 7, which had now been in orbit for 11 days. Each craft, for the other, was nothing more than a gleaming speck somewhere in all that vast blackness!

For more than five hours, Stafford worked with the spacecraft's built-in computer and radar, which gave Schirra the information for bringing Gemini 6 into the same area of space occupied by Gemini 7. Finally, Schirra beheld the gleaming cone shape of the other spacecraft in the distance. "There seems to be a lot of traffic up here," Schirra wisecracked to the people listening back on Earth.

Then Schirra began the ticklish job of bringing Gemini 6 in close to Gemini 7, as if he were going to dock with it. A burst of rocket fire from the rear of his craft to nudge it forward, a burst from the top to move it slightly down, and so on. The two vessels were moving nearly 18,000 miles an hour, the speed at which they had gone into orbit; but with no wind whistling past and with no weight, they hardly seemed to be moving at all. Each flare of Gemini 6's rockets seemed to provide a gentle thrust that made the craft "float" just a little faster. The distance closed to 100 feet, 80 feet, 50 feet. Skillfully, Schirra brought his craft to within 1 foot of the other! He and Stafford could see the grinning faces of Borman and Lovell looking at them from Gemini 7's portholes—faces that bore fuzzy beards, for the two Gemini 7 astronauts hadn't been able to shave during the 11 days they had been in space.

That meeting of Gemini 6 and Gemini 7 showed that a Gemini spacecraft could be maneuvered into a docking position with no trouble. All that remained was to try an actual docking. Within three months, the stage was set for that. An Agena target craft was launched into orbit, and on March 16, 1966, Gemini 8 followed it up. Astronaut Neil Armstrong was piloting, accompanied by astronaut David Scott. Some six hours after they had lifted off Earth, Armstrong and Scott guided Gemini 8 to the target and were only about 150 feet behind it.

Slowly, Armstrong eased Gemini 8 forward until its barrel-shaped nose was pushing into the flared cone at the Agena's tail. A ring inside the cone grasped the Gemini's nose. The two vessels were locked together, and for the first time in human history, a spacecraft was linked to another, in space.

The docking had been easy, but now something happened that reminded everyone the conquest of space wasn't always going to be easy. About half an hour after the Gemini had docked, one of its thrusters—the small rocket engines used to steer it—short-circuited and fired when it wasn't supposed to. The Gemini and the Agena, linked together, began to spin violently!

The astronauts' training covered such emergencies as this, and Armstrong did what he had to do. He backed the Gemini out of the Agena, shut off the faulty thruster, and immediately began to return to Earth. He and Scott landed safely a short time later.

So the Gemini 8 flight ended a lot earlier than it was supposed to and scared quite a few people for a while. But it had done what it set out to do. The question of whether a ship could dock in space had now been firmly answered.

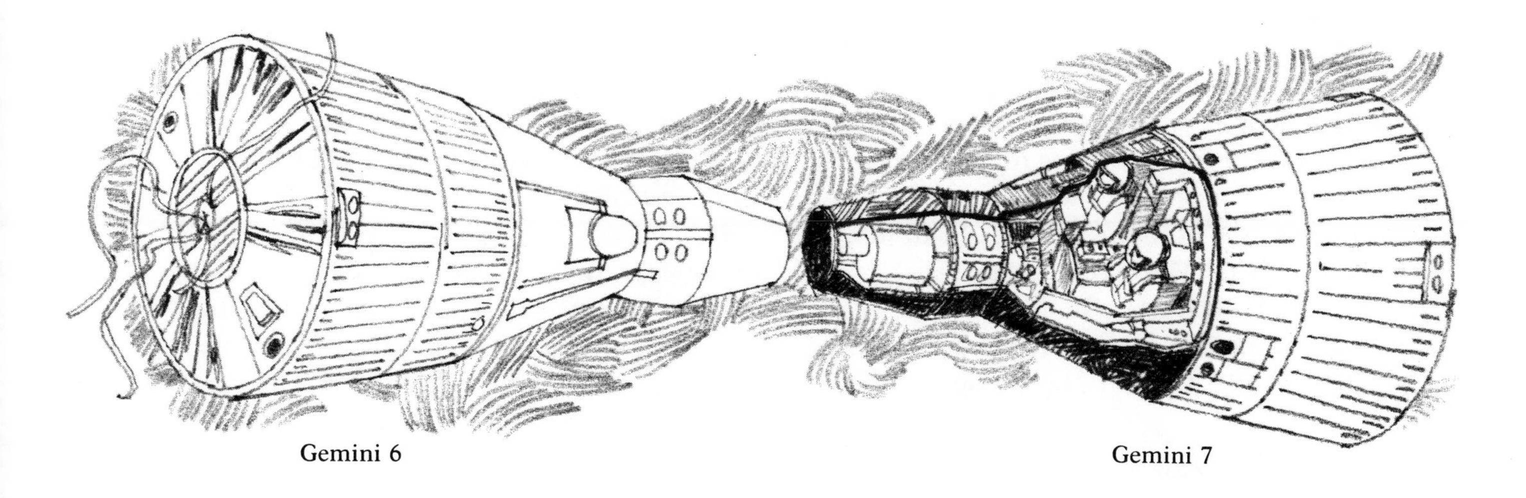

Gemini 6 Gemini 7

Reaching for the Moon

ON A DAY in September 1959, an object came hurtling out of the starry blackness of the Moon's sky and smashed onto one of the Moon's rocky, crater-scarred plains. This wasn't particularly unusual. During its billions of years of existence, the Moon has been struck by untold millions of meteoroids: chunks of rock the size of a grain of sand to the size of a respectable mountain. These meteoroids whiz about in parts of the Solar System and often smack into the various planets and moons. It was the force of many such impacts that pocked and pitted the Moon's surface with big and little craters.

But the object that struck the Moon that day in 1959 wasn't just another chunk of meteoric rock. It was a smooth, round metal ball filled with machinery—the first space vessel from Earth ever to land on another object in the Solar System. The people of Earth had reached across 240,000 miles to touch their nearest neighbor in space. It was a beginning step in making humanity's age-old dream of visiting the Moon come true.

For thousands upon thousands of years, people hadn't been able to do anything other than look at the Moon. With the invention of the telescope, over 370 years ago, people could see the Moon more closely. They could see that it was another world, with mountains, valleys, and what appeared to be wide seas (but later turned out to be great plains). However, even as telescopes were improved and the view of the Moon was brought closer, there was a host of questions that couldn't be answered just by looking. Did the Moon have an atmosphere? Were some of those craters that dotted its surface volcanoes? Even as recently as 50 years ago, most scientists felt these and similar questions could probably never be answered.

When spaceflight became a reality, everyone realized that now those questions could be answered. It was only a matter of time until human beings would actually go to the Moon and find out some of the answers themselves. But even before then, machines could be sent; machines that could take pictures and gather all kinds of information.

However, sending even an unmanned spacecraft to the Moon was going to be far harder than putting a spacecraft into orbit. A Moon-bound craft would have to travel at a much higher speed, which

The Moon

LUNA 2 CRASHES
ON THE MOON

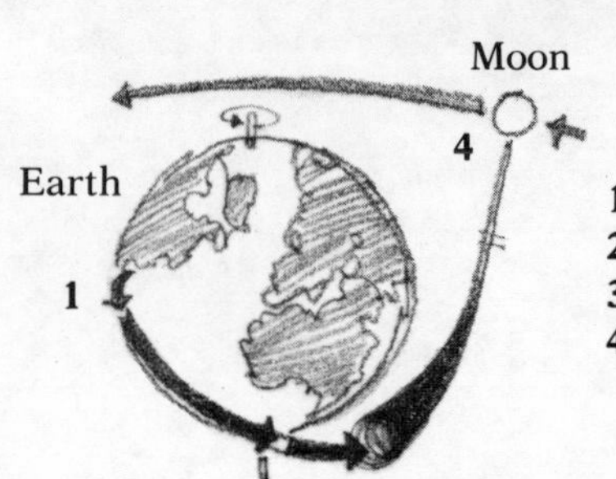

1 Ranger 7 is launched by Atlas–Agena rocket.
2 Craft coasts in Earth orbit.
3 Ranger enters 10-mile-wide "launch corridor."
4 Ranger reaches the Moon.

meant it would have to be carried into space by a bigger, more powerful first-stage booster rocket. And, of course, the Moon is always moving. To land on the Moon, a vessel would have to be aimed at where the Moon would be when the vessel got there. The slightest error could cause a miss.

The first attempt was launched from Russia on January 2, 1959. Called Luna 1—after Luna, the Latin name for the moon—it was a 4-foot-wide metal ball, studded with conical projections and with a number of slim rods sticking out of it. Its job was to find out what the conditions were in space close to the Moon. As it sped past the Moon within a distance of about 3,700 miles, its instruments sent back some important and useful information.

Eight months later, Luna 2 was launched. It was the object that crashed into the Moon that September day in 1959. By crashing, it did its job, which was to see if a spacecraft could be sent from Earth on a course that would bring it down on the Moon.

Luna 3, launched by the Soviets on October 4, 1959, showed the people of Earth a sight that no one had ever before seen. As the Moon moves in its orbit around Earth, one side of it—the same side—always faces Earth. Thus, no human had ever seen the other side of the Moon. But Luna 3 passed around the Moon, and its cameras took pictures of the Moon's other side. The pictures were automatically developed and then sent back to Earth by television. In one day, our knowledge of the Moon was literally doubled.

In the United States, in 1961, President John Kennedy announced that the nation's goal was actually to send people to land on the Moon by the year 1970. Thus, the scientists and technicians of the U.S. National Aeronautics and Space Administration—NASA—had a lot of work to do and a lot of questions to answer in less than ten years. For example, some astronomers believed the Moon's surface was so thickly covered with billions of years of dust that a spacecraft landing there might sink and be helplessly trapped. So the NASA scientists set up a plan to send a series of unmanned probes, or search, vessels to the Moon to land, to take pictures, to test the soil, and so on. The vessels were named Rangers.

From the beginning, the Ranger program was dogged with difficulties. Ranger 1 was launched for the Moon in August of 1961. It failed to gain a high-enough orbit and soon fell back, burning up in the atmosphere. Three months later, exactly the same thing happened to Ranger 2!

Corrections were made, and in January of 1962, Ranger 3 was launched. But it slipped off course, missed the Moon by more than 22,000 miles, and flew on to be lost in space forever.

More corrections were made. In April, Ranger 4 lifted off. Straight as an arrow, it headed for its target. But again something went wrong, and the NASA technicians found they had lost all contact with the probe. It crashed on the Moon, thus becoming the first U.S. spacecraft to get there. But no information was gained from it.

However, the scientists and technicians felt they now had most of the problems licked. With great hope, Ranger 5 was launched on October 18, 1962. Midway to the Moon, all its electrical batteries went dead. It went off course, missing the Moon, by 450 miles, and flew on into space.

More than a year passed before Ranger 6 was sent on its mission. Designed to take close-up pictures of the lunar surface starting at a distance of 900 miles, it contained six television cameras and two transmitters. Launched January 30, 1964, it headed straight for its target while scientists waited hopefully. But nothing happened. Not one of the cameras worked! Ranger 6 simply smashed into the Moon's surface.

Dejectedly, the NASA people went back to work to try and produce a foolproof system for turning on a probe's cameras and transmitting the pictures back to Earth. By July they felt they had it, and Ranger 7 was launched.

Ranger 7 broke free of Earth's gravity and sped into space on course. All of its automatic machinery was working perfectly. At a distance of 1,120 miles from the Moon, it began to take pictures. As it dropped ever nearer the Moon's surface, the pictures showed more and more detail, revealing that the apparently smooth plains of the Moon are actually pocked with billions of small craters. Once again, the people of Earth were seeing things never before seen by human eyes.

The Russians, too, were still sending probes to the Moon and also had some disappointing failures. But on February 3, 1966, came a spectacular Soviet success. An odd buglike machine, Luna 9, landed safely, without crashing, and sent back the first pictures ever taken on the Moon's surface.

Throughout the next few years, both the United States and the Soviet Union continued to add to their stores of knowledge about the Moon and how to get there. The eyes of the world were on this "space race" between the two nations. Who would win it? Which would be first to actually send men to the Moon?

On December 21, 1968, the world had part of its answer. Three American astronauts—Frank Borman, William Anders, and James Lovell—entered Apollo 8 and prepared for launching. They would be the first humans to orbit the Moon. One of the greatest of all human adventures and achievements was now about to begin!

Luna 9 on the Moon

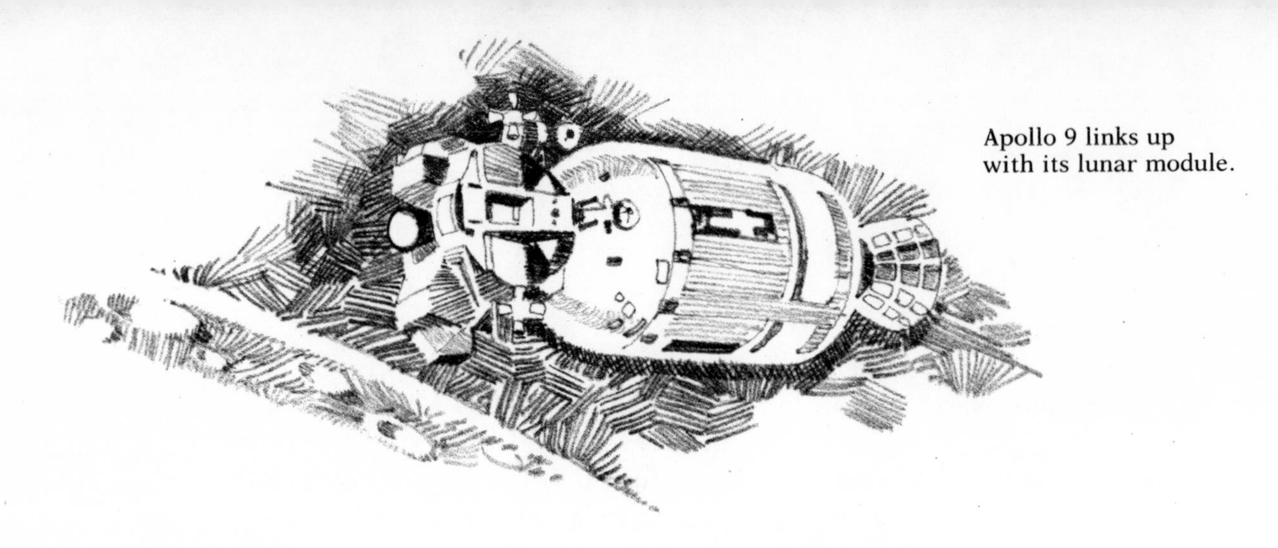

Apollo 9 links up with its lunar module.

Footprints on the Moon

THE COMMAND MODULE in which men rode *to* the Moon wasn't built to land *on* the Moon. The actual landing would be made by a special little squat, square, buglike craft known as an LM, which stood for *Lunar Module,* meaning "Moon Craft." The LM would be carried to the Moon on an Apollo, which would go into orbit around the Moon. The LM would be flown down to the Moon's surface by two astronauts and then flown back up to the Apollo. But before any of this could take place, the NASA people wanted to test everything and make sure it all worked!

The first test was the flight of Apollo 8, which carried astronauts Borman, Anders, and Lovell into orbit around the Moon. This showed that an Apollo could reach the Moon, orbit it, and then return to Earth without mishap.

Next came a test of disconnecting the LM from an Apollo and then linking up again. This was done in March of 1969 by astronauts James McDivitt, Russell Schweickart, and David Scott, aboard Apollo 9, orbiting Earth.

On May 18, 1969, Thomas Stafford, John Young, and Eugene Cernan were launched in Apollo 10. They tested the LM's flight action, actually taking it down to 8 miles above the Moon's surface. Everything went well. All was now ready for the actual landing on the Moon.

On the morning of July 16, 1969, a Saturn booster rocket lifted off the Cape Canaveral launchpad carrying Apollo 11 and its LM. On board the Apollo were Michael Collins, the pilot, and Neil Armstrong and Edwin "Buzz" Aldrin, who would land the LM on the Moon. The Apollo had been given the name Columbia, while the LM was called Eagle.

On July 20, as Columbia sped in orbit around the Moon, Armstrong and Aldrin entered the tiny LM. Slowly, Eagle, the LM, was separated from Columbia. A blast from one of its engines sent Eagle coursing down toward the Moon's surface. Actually, it was falling like a stone through the Moon's airless sky. But a steady blast from its big landing engine, pointing downward, was thrusting it upward, thus slowing its fall so that it would land without crashing. Back on Earth, people could hear Neil Armstrong's voice coming over the radio as he helped Eagle's pilot, Buzz Aldrin, land the LM.

"Down two and a half. Forward. For-

APOLLO 11 LANDS—FIRST MAN ON THE MOON

Saturn booster rocket carries Apollo 11 skyward.

"One small step for man . . ."

ward. Good. Forty feet. Down two and a half. Kicking up some dust. Thirty feet. Two and a half down. Faint shadow. Four forward. Drifting to the right a little. Contact light. Okay, engine stop."

Tense and silent, the people at NASA Mission Control, on Earth, waited. So many things could go wrong! If the descent was too fast, Eagle could crash. If the ground was too uneven, the craft could tip over after landing, and the two astronauts would be stranded—and doomed!

Then Armstrong's voice broke into the silence.

"Tranquility Base here. The Eagle has landed."

The dream of centuries had come true. Human beings were on the Moon!

Now the two astronauts began their preparations for walking on the Moon's surface. Finally, everything was ready. Armstrong reported that Eagle's hatch had been opened. Helped by Aldrin, he backed through the hatch onto a ladder. A television camera mounted on the outside of the LM began to work. On Earth, millions of people watched with awe and excitement as their TV screens showed the actual moment of a human stepping onto another world! They saw Armstrong, bulky in his space suit, standing on the slim ladder. They heard his voice.

"I'm at the foot of the ladder. The LM footpads are only depressed in the surface about one or two inches. I'm going to step off the LM now."

His left foot reached down, momentarily touched the ground, was pulled up again. Then it came down firmly onto the surface. A moment later, his right foot was placed beside it.

"That's one small step for man, one giant leap for mankind," he said.

A human being was standing on the Moon, 240,000 miles across empty space from where he had been born!

Armstrong walked about, leaving footprints in the fine, powdery dust that coated the Moon's surface. (The fear of the astronomers had been laid to rest; the dust wasn't deep enough to sink into.) In a few minutes, Armstrong was joined by Aldrin, who tested the Moon's gravity by running and jumping. To people watching on Earth, he seemed to be half-floating in slow motion, for the Moon's gravity is far less than that of Earth. The two men planted an American flag in the Moon's soil, then began the important work of setting up instruments for experiments and collecting samples of rock to be brought back to Earth for study.

Unknown to the astronauts and the millions of people watching on Earth, Mission Control scientists were working frantically to solve a serious and frightening problem. During Eagle's descent to the Moon, Mission Control had lost track of the craft for a short time. As a result, it wasn't known exactly where Eagle had landed. Without knowing Eagle's location, Mission Control could not figure out the exact amount of time Eagle's engine would have to fire in order to put the ship on the proper path to rejoin Columbia,

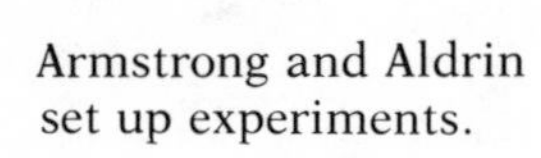

Armstrong and Aldrin set up experiments.

Collecting Samples
With a Lunar Scoop

orbiting overhead! The astronauts were in grave danger! Fortunately, when the time came for Eagle to leave, the problem had been solved.

Eagle had been built so that its bottom section would now become a launching platform from which the top portion, carrying the two astronauts, would take off. Affixed to the bottom was a metal plate on which were engraved the words,

HERE MEN FROM THE PLANET EARTH
FIRST SET FOOT UPON THE MOON,
JULY 1969, A.D.
WE CAME IN PEACE FOR ALL MANKIND

Thus, when the upper portion of Eagle blasted off, this plate stayed behind. With no rain or wind to affect it, it will never damage or wear away. It will be there on the Moon for millions of years.

Eagle sped up from the Moon's surface on an arrowhead of flame from its takeoff engine. Inside Columbia, moving steadily in orbit around the Moon, astronaut Collins saw Eagle's blinking beacon light coming toward him. The two vessels linked—a tribute to all the many docking operations that had gone before—and Armstrong and Aldrin, with their boxes of Moon rocks, went back aboard Columbia. Eagle was then cast loose, to save weight and conserve fuel for the return trip. A short time later, Columbia's engine flared, starting the spaceship toward Earth.

And so what many people consider to be humanity's greatest adventure came to an end. But it was really more of a beginning. From 1969 to 1972, there were five more landings on the Moon. Men from Earth explored the surface, collected more samples of rock, took thousands of pictures, performed valuable experiments, and even traveled over the Moon's surface in a special sort of car called a Lunar Rover. We learned more about the Moon in those few short years than we had been able to learn in all the thousands of years before.

But there's still a lot to learn, a lot of questions yet to be answered, a lot more exploring to be done. People of Earth will go to the Moon again in the future. And perhaps you'll be one of them!

Astronauts ride in a "moonmobile," the Lunar Rover.

Mars' Rocky Surface

Looking at the Red Planet

TOWARD THE END of the last century, the planet Mars suddenly attracted special attention. An astronomer thought he saw a number of dark lines crisscrossing the surface of Mars. Many people believed these lines were canals that had been dug by intelligent beings. The idea that there were living creatures on Mars became common.

From what we could tell from Earth, in the days just before spaceflight, it certainly seemed as if Mars could support life. Through telescopes it could be seen that Mars's north and south poles are covered with ice, just like the poles of Earth. This showed there could be water on the planet. And at times, large parts of Mars seemed to grow darker, stay dark for a time, then fade—as if large areas of plant life were blooming, growing, then dying, just as on Earth. Thus, when the United States announced it was sending probe craft to Mars, many people waited hopefully to learn about life on the Red Planet.

The first spacecraft to reach Mars was a U.S. Mariner, which looked like four windmill vanes with an eight-sided box hanging beneath them and a shiny bowl mounted above. The vanes were solar panels. They would soak up sunlight and turn it into electrical power to run the Mariner's machinery, most of which was inside the eight-sided box. The shiny bowl was an antenna for sending information back to Earth. This Mariner was labeled Mariner 4.

Mariner 4 was launched on November 28, 1964. Reaching Mars on July 15, 1965, after a journey of more than seven months, the spacecraft passed over the Red Planet and took a series of 22 pictures, relayed back to Earth.

The pictures were a shock! They showed that the surface of Mars apparently has many craters, like the surface of the Moon. No one had ever suspected such a thing. Obviously, if Mars were like the Moon, it certainly couldn't support life. However, Mariner's pictures really showed only a very tiny portion of the surface of Mars, and everyone agreed more information was needed before the idea of life had to be abandoned.

It wasn't until 1969, when Mariner 6 and Mariner 7 were launched, a month apart, that Earth gained new knowledge of the Red Planet. The two Mariners sent back a total of 195 pictures, together with

MARINER 4 SPEEDS PAST MARS

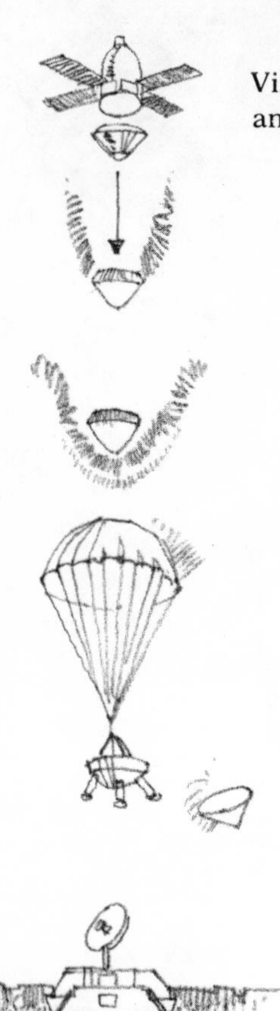

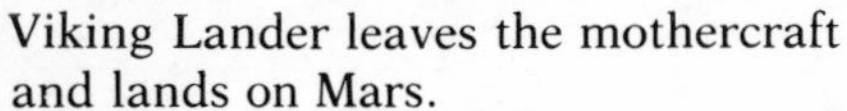

Viking Lander leaves the mothercraft and lands on Mars.

information about Mars's temperature, atmosphere, and surface. This information indicated that Mars was quite different from the Moon and Earth. The pictures showed it to be a cold, dry, desert world with oddly jumbled ridges and valleys, spotted with ancient craters. Instruments showed it had a thin atmosphere of carbon dioxide gas, and the ice covering its two poles seemed to be frozen carbon dioxide. (On Earth, frozen carbon dioxide is known as dry ice and can only be made artificially.) There were no canals in any of the pictures, and it didn't look as if such a place could support life. Yet there was a chance, many scientists agreed, that Mars could support some kind of simple, rugged life form very different from anything known on Earth—not a big creature, but perhaps microbes, or "germs," living in the soil.

The next American spacecraft and several Soviet spacecraft launched for Mars were largely failures. Then the Soviet Mars 3 craft, launched on May 28, 1971, made a successful landing on the Red Planet, although it "went dead" immediately afterward. The U.S. Mariner 9, launched two days later, became the first craft to go into orbit around Mars. Mariner 9 sent back over 7,000 pictures of the surface—including one of what appeared to be a dry riverbed, one of an enormous volcano, and one of a gigantic canyon as long as the width of North America!

The United States began building two special spacecraft. These were designed to land on Mars, test the atmosphere from top to bottom, send back the first pictures taken from the Martian surface, and perform experiments to find out, once and for all, if there was life on the Red Planet.

The two craft were known as Viking 1 and Viking 2. A Viking resembled a Mariner, but was considerably larger. It also carried something extra. Beneath the eight-sided box was a large "bowl," inside which was a lander, or landing craft, designed to go down onto the surface of Mars and do a number of things there. The lander was actually a miniature automatic laboratory. The Viking would be carried inside a Centaur D-1T spacecraft for the 212-million-mile journey to Mars, and the Centaur would be launched into space by a Titan IIIE booster rocket.

Viking 1 was launched August 20, 1975. Ten months later it went into orbit around the Red Planet. Its cameras began sending back pictures of a rugged, cratered surface. On Earth, scientists studied the pictures for three weeks before they found a place that looked smooth enough for Viking's lander. On July 20, 1976, the signal to land was sent across space from Earth. The lander separated from the rest of the craft, which continued in orbit, taking pictures and acting as a relay station for transmitting information from the lander back to Earth.

A built-in computer on the lander now took control. It fired rocket engines that sent the lander speeding down toward the planet. As the lander entered the Martian atmosphere, the protective shell around it was seared by friction, but the precious machine inside was unharmed. About 19,000 feet from the surface, a parachute opened, slowing the lander's fall. The shell was then automatically jettisoned, or cast loose. Later, the parachute was also jettisoned. At 4,600 feet, rocket engines flared again, slowing the descent to only 4 miles an hour. At that speed, the lander settled onto the surface of Mars.

The TV cameras on the lander began to swing slowly from left to right, taking panoramic, or wide, pictures of the landscape. On Earth, the pictures built up, one thin horizontal strip at a time, on TV screens at the Jet Propulsion Laboratory in California. Taken in black-and-white, through filters, they were reconstructed in color by computer. They showed a broad section of rusty-colored, boulder-strewn desert under an orange sky. Picture after picture, combined with information from other instruments on the lander and the orbiter, showed that Mars is a bitterly cold desert, spotted with patches of frost during the Martian winter. The ice that covers Mars's north pole turned out to be a layer of carbon dioxide "frost" over thick frozen water. Mars is a world in an ice age!

The experiment to see if there was life on Mars began on July 28. It was controlled from Earth by means of radio waves. A long metal "arm" reached out from the lander and dug up small amounts of red Martian soil. The soil was carried back inside the lander, where instruments went to work to find out if any living microbes were in it. The soil was heated, moistened with a broth that microbes could use for food, then tested to see if it gave off gases or radiation—which it would if microbes were present.

As results of these tests were sent back to Earth, there was a flurry of excitement among scientists. The soil seemed to be producing gas! However, none of the other signs of life were showing up. It was most mysterious.

On August 7, Viking 2 arrived over Mars, and on September 3, its lander descended. More marvelous pictures and information were sent to Earth, and the lander performed the same sorts of experiments on the soil that Viking 1 had. But the same things happened. Most scientists finally decided that the Martian soil is just chemically active, but that there probably is no life in it.

And so, we now know that Mars is a cold, red, desert world with towering mountains, titanic chasms, frozen water, and frequent dust storms. Even though it probably is lifeless, it's still an interesting and exciting place!

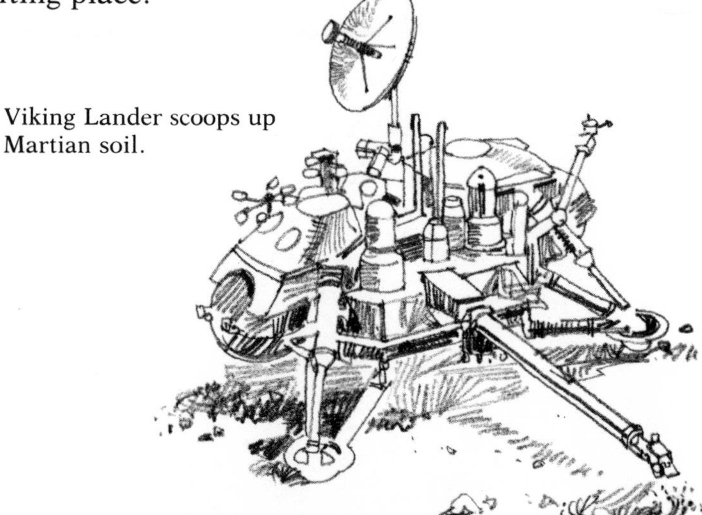

Viking Lander scoops up Martian soil.

The Mysteries of Earth's "Twin"

THE DEVICE LOOKED like nothing so much as a giant metal lightbulb with a bewildering array of curved tubes, rods, struts, and machinery affixed to it. Carried by a "mother ship," it had been moving steadily across 185 million miles of space, a journey of four months, and now it had reached its destination. Below it hung a huge, cloudy, yellowish-brown ball—the planet Venus.

The device, labeled Venera 13 by the Russian scientists and technicians who had built and launched it, now automatically separated from the larger craft that had brought it here. The mother ship swung into orbit around the planet. Venera began to drop toward the planet's surface.

Had there been any human eyes looking down out of Venera, they would have seen nothing but swirling mist, for Venus is wrapped in a thick, cloudy atmosphere that completely hides its surface. Into that soupy mist Venera now plunged at a speed of about 7 miles a second, slowing somewhat from the friction of moving through an atmosphere 90 times more dense than the atmosphere of Earth. Venera 13 was hissing through "air" that was heavy carbon dioxide gas and sliding through clouds composed of stinging droplets of sulfuric acid. The Venusian atmosphere is deadly!

Six large parachutes, automatically flopped out of the top of Venera and billowed open in turn. The spacecraft's fall slowed to a gentle drift through the swirling gloom. As Venera drifted downward, sensitive instruments built into it were measuring the pressure and temperature of the atmosphere and the makeup of its gases. This information was being instantly relayed by radio signals to the mother ship overhead. The mother ship, in turn, was relaying it back across the millions of miles to Earth.

Finally, a little more than an hour after entering the atmosphere, Venera landed on a bleak, rocky, rust-colored landscape beneath a murky orange sky flickering with lightning bolts. The force of the landing raised a small cloud of dust. One after another, TV cameras mounted on Venera began to take pictures of the surroundings through red, green, and blue filters. From these, computers on Earth would be able to determine the actual color of the landscape. A drilling device reached down

VENERA 13 LANDS ON VENUS

Information is received from Mariner 5.

from Venera and bit into the ground. A small sample of rock was dug out and carried back inside, where machinery put the rock through tests to determine what it was made of. All of this information, too, was being radioed up to the circling mother ship and relayed back to Earth. The secrets of Venus were being revealed.

Until the space age began, Venus was a complete mystery. Because it is almost exactly the same size as Earth, it was often called Earth's "twin." Of all the planets, it comes closest to Earth in distance. But even as recently as 1960, there was no way to tell what lay under its cloudy atmosphere or what that atmosphere was composed of. Some astronomers thought the surface of Venus might be a giant desert and that the cloudy atmosphere was mainly windblown dust. Others thought the atmosphere was carbon dioxide gas and Venus's surface was covered with a huge ocean. Still others thought the atmosphere was a kind of thick smog and the surface was covered with an ocean of oil!

Within less than five years after the world's first spacecraft, Sputnik 1, had been launched, both the United States and the Soviet Union began making attempts to solve the mysteries of Venus. In February of 1961, a Soviet craft labeled *Venera*—meaning "Venus"—1 passed within 62,000 miles of Venus. A year later, the U.S. Mariner 2 passed within 22,000 miles. Venera 3, launched from Russia in 1965, became the first spacecraft to reach Venus, crashing on the surface. These were all partial successes, but there were also a number of failures.

Then came some real successes and some valuable information. In October of 1967, Soviet and American spacecraft arrived at Venus within a day of each other. Arriving first, the Soviet Venera 4, resembling a legless insect body with a pair of rectangular wings, hanging beneath a giant bowl, entered the Venusian atmosphere. The back portion of the craft, a round ball filled with instruments, automatically separated from the rest. A parachute snapped open over it, and it floated down to the planet's surface. During this drop, which took about 90 minutes, the instruments radioed information that was relayed to Earth. The instruments indicated that the atmosphere of Venus is almost entirely carbon dioxide gas with a tiny amount of oxygen and water vapor, that Venus's atmosphere is much thicker than Earth's atmosphere, and that Venus is quite hot—from 104 to 536 degrees Fahrenheit!

The next day, the U.S. Mariner 5, looking like an eight-sided box hanging from windmill vanes, sped past Venus at a distance of less than 2,500 miles. Its instruments showed that Venus, unlike Earth, has almost no magnetic field, or magnetism.

During 1970 and 1972, two U.S.S.R. Veneras made landings on Venus, and the U.S. Mariner 10 went past Venus and the planet Mercury, taking pictures of both. The Venus pictures showed only swirling clouds, and the Mercury pictures showed that this planet, the closest to the Sun, is a great deal like Earth's Moon.

In October of 1975, a landing capsule from Venera 9 landed on Venus and took the first photo of the surface. The picture showed rocks and smooth boulders strewn about on rocky ground. Venera 9's instruments also showed that the temperature of the surface where the craft had landed was more than 900 degrees Fahrenheit—hot enough to melt lead! A short time later another Venera, Venera 10, dropped a landing capsule that sent back another picture of rocky, desertlike landscape. The instruments of both craft also provided information on the amount of sunlight that manages to reach Venus's surface through the thick clouds, the speeds of the winds that whip through the atmosphere, and the makeup of the Venusian soil.

In 1978, the United States launched Pioneer Venus 1, a round "box" full of instruments. Pioneer Venus 1 went into orbit around Venus, taking pictures and making a map of the surface by means of radar. Not long after, Pioneer Venus 2, a round box with four squat cones sticking out of its top, came speeding out of space. Each of the cones was actually a separate probe craft, which detached and went shooting into the Venusian atmosphere with instruments measuring, recording, and transmitting back to Earth. Later, in 1978, two more Soviet ships, Venera 11 and Venera 12, landed on Venus. And then in 1981, Venera 13 and Venera 14 were sent.

Thus, during the 20 years since Venera 1—the first Venus probe—was launched, scientists were able to put together a picture of Earth's "twin," a little bit at a time. It is a world that's a sizzling hot, rocky desert, gashed in places with gigantic chasms and studded in others with ranges of towering mountains, some of which are volcanoes. Several huge plateaus rise above the rest of the surface, like great continents. The daylight sky above the desert is a ruddy orange, and it is filled with flickers of lightning. The sulfuric-acid clouds high above the desert are whipped by winds more powerful than the most powerful hurricane that ever blew on Earth. Yet although Venus now hardly seems like a twin to our world, there is evidence that it may once have been a good deal more like Earth. It may once have had a great ocean—and perhaps there were living things in that ocean!

So Venus is no longer the puzzling mystery it was to us less than 30 years ago. The mystery was solved by the age of spaceflight!

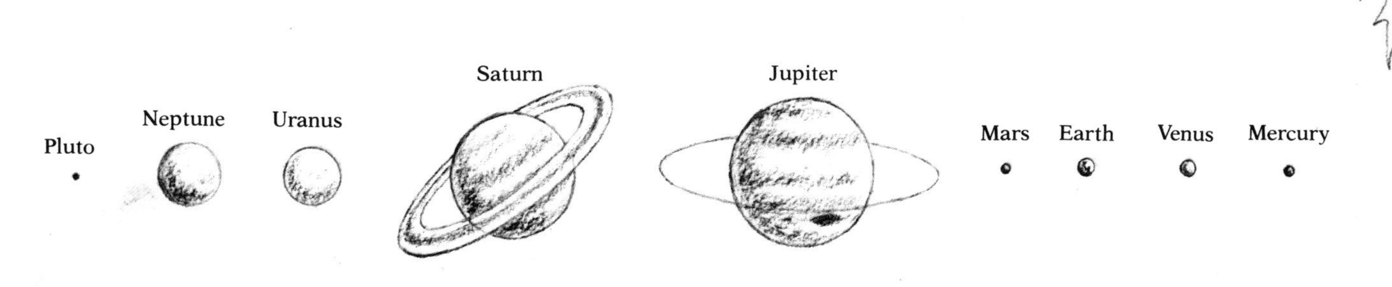

Venus and Earth are second and third closest to the Sun.

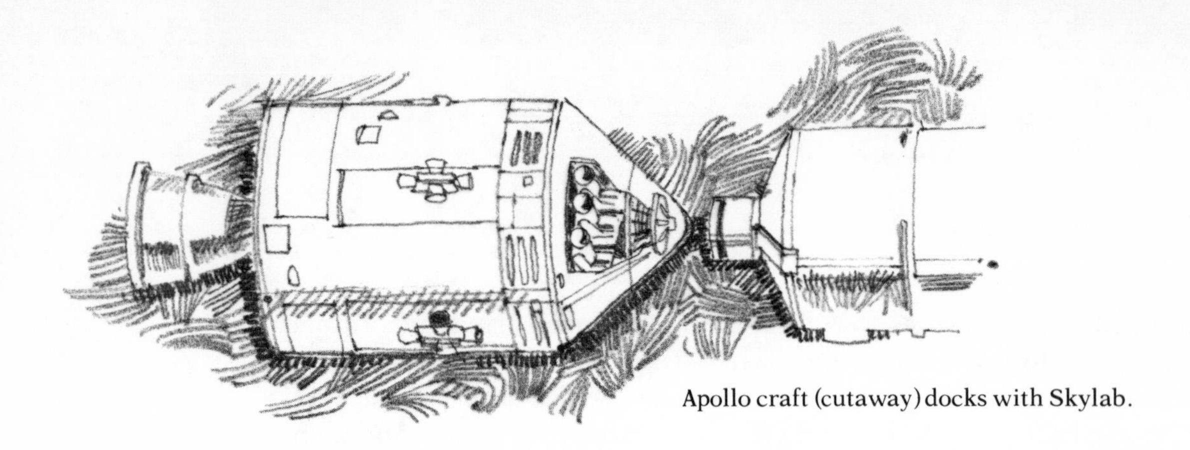

Apollo craft (cutaway) docks with Skylab.

A Repair Job in Space

IT WAS MAY 14, 1973. With a ground-shaking roar, an American Saturn 5 rocket lifted off the launchpad in Florida and hurtled skyward. Its third stage was a 118-foot-long, instrument-packed cylinder that was designed to be a laboratory in space. Named Skylab, it would orbit Earth, and crews of astronauts would live and work in it for months at a time. The first crew was to be sent up the next day.

But as Skylab sped through Earth's atmosphere, disaster struck! A thin metal shield, designed to protect part of the craft from the impact of tiny meteorites and from the fierce heat of the Sun in space, ripped loose and went whirling away. As the shield tore loose, it caused still other damage. Skylab had two "wings" that were actually power-supply units for turning sunlight into electricity. These wings were folded against Skylab's sides until it went into orbit. But the ripping away of the shield pulled open one wing partway, and left a strip of metal across the other wing, pinning it, so that it couldn't open. When a rocket engine automatically fired a short time later, the blast caused the partly opened wing to break off and go spinning away into the darkness of space.

Skylab went into orbit, and its automatic machinery went to work. A framework holding eight special telescopes unfolded in the direction of the Sun. Four small power-supply wings, resembling the vanes of a windmill, opened up. But with one of the main power wings gone and the other unable to open, Skylab did not have enough power for all its machinery, lights, heat, and air conditioning. With the shield gone, sunlight was beating directly on the craft. Its interior was rapidly becoming too hot for humans to live in, while its supplies of food, medicine, and other perishables would soon be ruined by the heat. In orbit 270 miles above Earth, Skylab was badly crippled and in serious danger of becoming a useless hulk!

It was obvious that if Skylab was to be saved, it would have to be repaired. Such repairs could only be done by people in space suits working outside Skylab. This was just the sort of emergency scientists had foreseen many years earlier when they had astronauts make space walks to see if human beings could work effectively

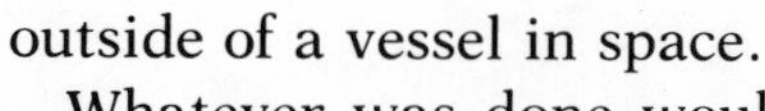

Skylab (cutaway) Beneath Saturn 5 Launch Cover

outside of a vessel in space.

Whatever was done would have to be done soon, for the longer Skylab was left in its present condition, the worse that condition would get. So engineers and technicians sweated to think quickly of something to replace the missing sun shield and some way to free the stuck wing.

Days went by. A week went by. Finally, on May 25, 11 days after Skylab's disastrous launch, an Apollo spacecraft, boosted into orbit by a Saturn 1B rocket, headed toward the stricken Skylab. Aboard were three astronauts: Charles Conrad, Jr.; Joseph P. Kerwin; and Paul J. Weitz; all officers of the U.S. Navy. They were to be Skylab's first crew. But first, they'd have to fix it!

With Charles Conrad, the commander, piloting, the Apollo locked briefly into the round "dock" opening at Skylab's rear, then undocked and maneuvered around Skylab. The astronauts looked over the damage. They made an attempt to unjam the power wing without actually going outside their craft—by standing in the air lock and reaching out. But that didn't work. Conrad then guided the Apollo back to docking position, only to run into another problem. The latches didn't lock as they should have, and it took five tries before he was able to lock the craft into place. It was now almost 15 hours since the exhausted astronauts had left Earth; they slept, in the cramped quarters of the Apollo.

Next day, Weitz and Conrad went through the front opening in the Apollo and entered Skylab. They wore their space suits to protect themselves from the heat, and they carried a device to take the place of the missing shield—a kind of giant umbrella made of tough plastic. Opening a porthole on the side of Skylab that faced the Sun, they pushed out the umbrella and opened it. Immediately, the terrible heat that had blistered Skylab's side with a temperature of more than 300 degrees Fahrenheit was blocked off. The interior of the space laboratory began to grow cooler.

But there still wouldn't be enough power until the pinned wing could be freed. A little over a week later, standing outside on Skylab's hull with the vast blue-and-white globe of Earth rolling beneath them, Conrad and Kerwin struggled to free the wing, using a pair of metal-cutting shears attached to a long pole. With these they managed to cut the metal strap that pinned the wing against the hull. And then, by simply attaching a line to the wing and hauling on it, they were able to pull the wing upright. Down on Earth, at the Mission Control Center in Texas, instruments began to show that Skylab's power output was increasing. The repair job was a success, and Skylab was saved! With the huge, strange-looking square umbrella keeping it cool and its one wing furnishing most of the power, the laboratory in space was now ready to do its job.

The Skylab crew settled down to work. Their "workshop" was an area 27 feet

Saturn 5 Rocket

long by 22 feet wide, with storage containers for food, water, and scientific equipment. At one end was the crew's living quarters, which was nothing more than a small table with built-in heaters for canned and frozen food and three sleeping bags arranged against the walls. There was also a special toilet, designed to work without gravity.

One of the main jobs was simply to find out how to live in space. There were problems that people on Earth don't have! Every time a drawer was opened, everything in it started to float away! The men themselves quickly got used to floating about and found themselves turning floating cartwheels and flip-flops to get from place to place. They also found they had to shout when they talked; for in Skylab's thin atmosphere, sound didn't carry as well as it does on Earth.

On June 22, after 28 days in space, the three astronauts reentered the Apollo spacecraft in which they had come to Skylab, and they blasted off back to Earth. Their stay in space had been a huge success. They had taken scores of photographs and made important observations with instruments.

In July of 1973, another three-man crew rocketed up to Skylab. This crew lived aboard the orbiting laboratory for 59 days, returning to Earth in September. A little over a month later, Skylab's third crew went up, staying in space for 84 straight days. These men returned to Earth in February of 1974.

Skylab's job was now finished. No more Earthlings would ever set foot in it. But the work that had been done aboard the laboratory in space, by the nine men who made up the crews, was of tremendous importance in a number of ways. A vast amount of new information had been gained about both the Sun and Earth, and there had been important findings for the field of medical science. Some of the experiments the astronauts had done showed it would be possible to manufacture certain things in space more cheaply and easily than on Earth. Perhaps most important of all, it had been proved that humans could live and work for long periods in space without any serious health or mental problems.

In 1979, Skylab's orbit began to "decay," meaning that the craft was dropping closer to Earth. Soon gravity would gain control of it, and it would come plunging down through the atmosphere, burning up from friction as it came. In July of 1979, this happened. Most of the big space vessel burned up long before it could reach the ground, but a small portion of it fell into a remote part of Australia.

So Skylab came to an end. But it had played a major part in humankind's slow movement out into space.

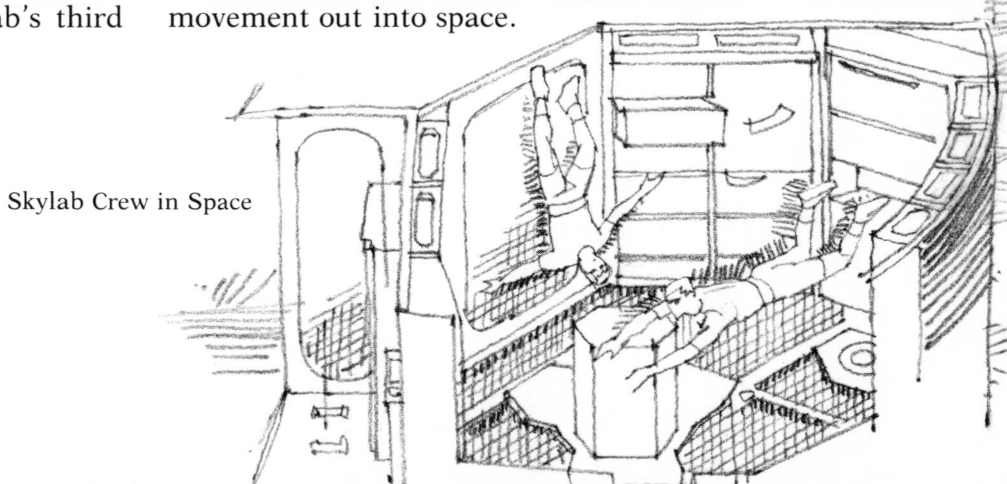

Skylab Crew in Space

Pioneer 10 in the Asteroid Belt

The Far Travelers

THE SPACECRAFT KNOWN as Pioneers were developed for investigating parts of space close to Earth. But scientists saw that with a few changes a Pioneer could be used for exploring some of the farther planets. So in 1972, a Pioneer spacecraft bearing the number 10 was launched toward the Solar System's fifth planet, Jupiter, some 390 million miles from Earth at its closest point.

Jupiter, the largest of all the planets, is a huge ball of *liquid* about 11 times bigger than Earth, possesses a thick atmosphere, and is orbited by some 16 moons. Astronomers had a lot of questions about it, such as: What caused the "Great Red Spot" that can be seen in its clouds? Pioneer 10 was sent to find out about that and other things.

Pioneer 10 resembled a 9-foot-wide metal umbrella with a long, thin pole and two metal-tube "arms" sticking out from beneath it. It was launched in the nose cone of a big Atlas-Centaur booster rocket. When separated from all the other stages, outside Earth's atmosphere, Pioneer 10 was moving at 9 miles a second—faster than anything else sent into space up to that time. But even at that speed, it took nearly two years to reach Jupiter!

Actually, astronomers weren't at all sure that Pioneer 10 would get to Jupiter. For between Mars and Jupiter lies the asteroid belt: a 120-million-mile-wide zone of thousands of chunks of rock, all wheeling in orbit around the Sun. Some of these rock chunks are more than 100 miles wide, and some are no more than the size of a pea. Pioneer 10 would be moving through this barrage of space hail for some seven months. Would it be able to get through without being struck and damaged, or even destroyed?

One hundred thirty-five days after its launching, Pioneer 10 entered the asteroid belt. During all the time it took to get through the belt, its instruments reported no encounters with any asteroids, big or little. Thus, it was clear that the asteroid belt was not going to be any danger to future spacecraft that would have to go through it.

On December 3, 1973, Pioneer 10 sped past Jupiter. It came within about 80,000 miles of the giant planet. It took photographs, made measurements, checked temperatures and radiation. The information it sent back across space to Earth pro-

PIONEER 10 PASSES JUPITER

Volcano erupts on Io, one of Jupiter's moons.

vided a breathtaking look at an awesome place. We learned that winds of 300 miles an hour roar through Jupiter's thick, cloudy atmosphere, and gigantic bolts of lightning that could burn an entire city to a cinder snake through the clouds. As for the Great Red Spot, it turned out to be an enormous sort of super-hurricane that's been swirling in Jupiter's atmosphere for centuries and may keep going for centuries more!

Leaving Jupiter behind, Pioneer 10 continued on a path that will take it into *interstellar* space—the incredibly vast area between stars. In another 120,000 years, Pioneer 10 will have traveled just about as far as the distance from the Sun to the nearest star.

In November of 1974, Pioneer 11, a duplicate of Pioneer 10, arrived at Jupiter, passing the giant planet at a distance of only 26,000 miles and gathering more information. But when Pioneer 11's task was finished, it took a different path. It headed toward Saturn, the sixth planet of the Solar System, more than 400 million miles beyond Jupiter.

The two Pioneers had given us a treasury of information about Jupiter, but they had really been rather poorly equipped for their job. However, the United States was now building two spacecraft especially designed for exploring the farther-out planets of the Solar System. These were the famous Voyagers. They resembled the Pioneers but were larger and carried more instruments.

The two Voyagers were launched in late summer of 1977, 16 days apart. Voyager 1 was actually launched after Voyager 2 but was given a speed and a trajectory that brought it to Jupiter first, in March of 1979. It swung past the fifth planet at a distance of 174,000 miles, and as it began to move away, its path carried it close to four of the largest of Jupiter's moons to take pictures and get information about them. Voyager 2 arrived about four months later, its path bringing it past the same moons as it approached Jupiter so that it was able to get pictures of their other sides.

Each Voyager took more than 15,000 pictures and performed special experiments. These increased our knowledge of Jupiter in a number of ways, such as the startling discovery that Jupiter is surrounded by a thin ring, apparently formed of orbiting rocks and dust. They also gave us our first real look at some of Jupiter's moons. Most of them are strange mixtures of rock and ice; and one, named Io, is dotted with active, erupting volcanoes.

The two Voyagers' routes had been carefully planned so each craft would be "kicked" by Jupiter's gravity onto a new path toward the planet Saturn. Saturn, more than 760 million miles from Earth at its closest point, is the second largest planet. Astronomers knew a few things about it, such as its rings are formed of chunks of ice or snow, and it has a number of moons. But for the most part, it was more of a mystery than Jupiter.

Of course, Pioneer 11, traveling far ahead of the two Voyagers, reached Saturn first, in September of 1979—6½ years after leaving Earth. The information it sent back to Earth included the fact that Saturn, like Jupiter, has an upside-down magnetic field, so that on Saturn a compass needle would point south instead of north. Pioneer also discovered one and possibly two new Saturnian moons and one more ring than could be seen from Earth.

When Voyager 1 arrived at Saturn in November of 1980, it provided an even more astounding look at the ringed planet and its satellites. For one thing, astronomers had thought Saturn had only six or seven rings of different widths, with gaps between them. But Voyager's pictures showed that each of the inner rings is actually made up of many thin rings, one inside another, so that there are really thousands of rings in all! As for Saturn itself, Voyager 1 found that its atmosphere is torn by winds even faster and more fierce than those on Jupiter.

Voyager 1's cameras also sent pictures of 12 of Saturn's moons, showing sights that couldn't have been imagined on Earth. On the moon Tethys is a 40-mile-wide, 465-mile-long valley, and a gigantic crater nearly one-fourth of the diameter of the moon Mimas. Voyager 1 also examined Titan, a very large, 3,180-mile-wide moon that has an atmosphere. Voyager 1 found the atmosphere to be mainly nitrogen gas. Unfortunately, the surface of Titan couldn't be seen because of a thick orange "smog" that fills the atmosphere of Titan.

Voyager 1 completed its mission and moved on, heading out of the Solar System. A year later, in August of 1981, Voyager 2 showed up. It added a great deal to the information gathered by Voyager 1. Then, in January of 1986, it swung past the Solar System's seventh planet, Uranus, which is 1 billion, 700 million miles from Earth. It found that Uranus has an Earth-size core of rock covered by an ocean 5,000 miles deep, and a thick atmosphere. It has 11 dark rings and ten moons formed of rock and ice. In 1989, Voyager 2 will pass the eighth planet, Neptune, and may be able to send us some facts about that far-distant world.

Thus, although the far travelers have already brought us a tremendous wealth of information, there may be much more yet to come. The Pioneers and Voyagers, those small, odd-looking machines speeding silently through the endless darkness, are literally the greatest explorers in human history!

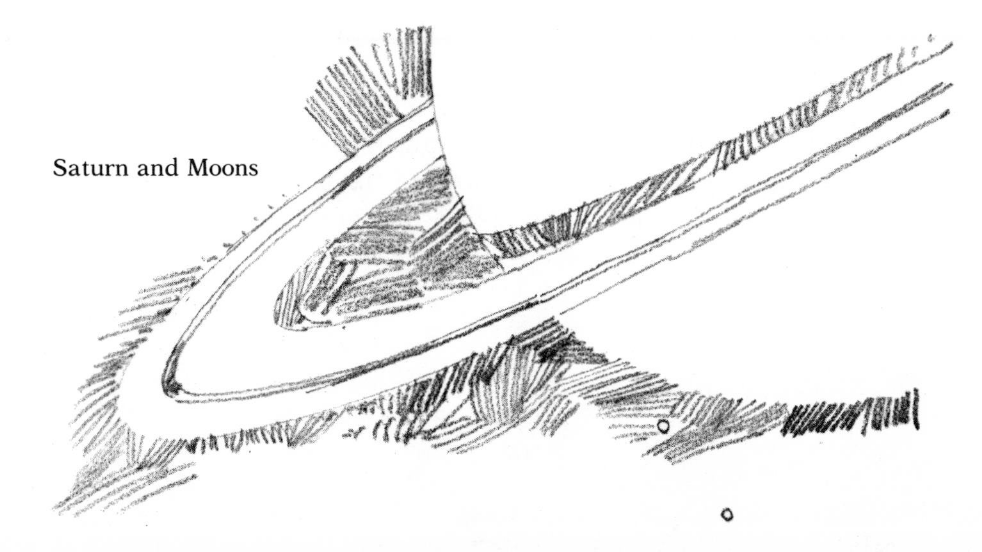
Saturn and Moons

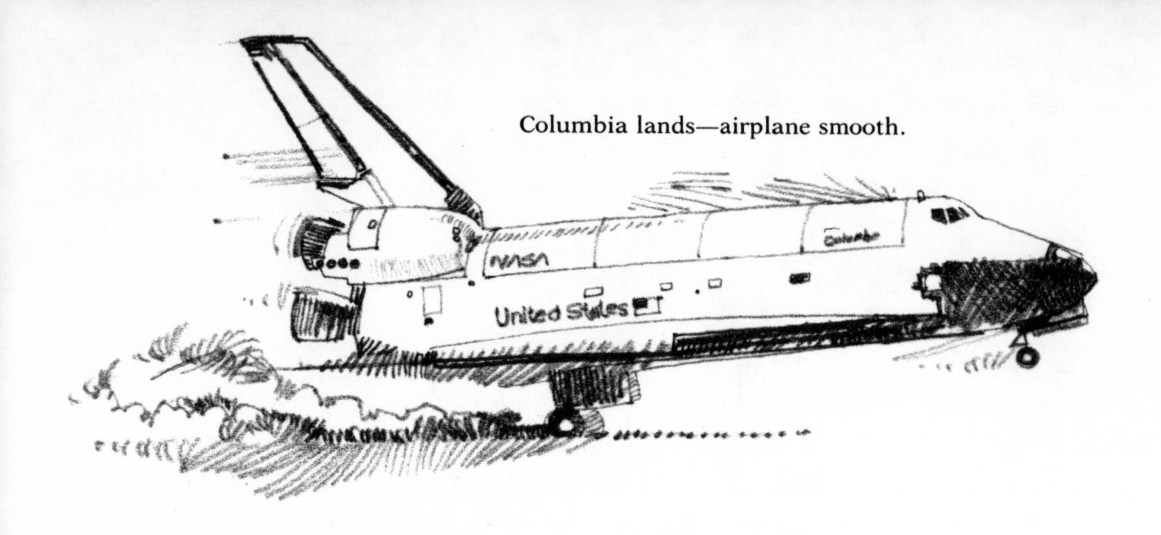

Columbia lands—airplane smooth.

The Space Shuttles

THE AIR of the California desert was shattered by a thundering sonic boom. A white dot was rushing toward Earth out of the clear blue sky. Nearer it came, revealing itself as a massive airplane with stubby, swept-back wings. Gradually slowing to a speed of 214 miles an hour—far, far faster than any jet aircraft coming in for a landing—the gleaming white craft touched its wheels neatly to the sand and came to a long, rolling stop. The space shuttle Columbia had returned from two days in orbit. It was the first spacecraft to *fly* back to Earth from space.

The Columbia was the first of the U.S. space program's space shuttles. It was launched on April 12, 1981, exactly 20 years from the day Yuri Gagarin made the first manned spaceflight in the tiny, ball-shaped Vostok 1. But Columbia was as different from Vostok as a modern jet airplane is from a hot-air balloon. It was the beginning of a new generation of spacecraft, actually a kind of combination rocket ship and airplane.

Columbia was a roomy, 122-foot-long vehicle with wings and a tail and plenty of space to carry cargo. It looked like an airplane, but it was launched like other spacecraft, by means of thundering rocket engines. It was fastened "piggyback" onto a gigantic torpedo-shaped liquid fuel tank that furnished the fuel for its main engines. Attached to the sides of the tank were two long, slim solid-fuel rockets. Steam billowed and flame spurted as this ungainly-looking construction first thundered skyward, lifted toward space by a total 6½ million pounds of *push* from its engines and the two rocket boosters. When the fuel in the two boosters was used up, they were detached and dropped back to Earth by parachute, to be used again in future launches. Minutes later, the empty liquid fuel tank was also detached, but no attempt was made to preserve it, and it broke into fragments that burnt up as they hurtled down through the atmosphere.

Columbia, now in space, went into orbit, made some tests, and then, two days after launching, began to return to Earth. It was turned so that its tail pointed forward, and its engines were fired to slow it and push it down toward Earth. As it fell toward Earth it began to glow red-hot from friction, but it was covered with heat-resistant tiles, and although a few of these had been knocked off during the

COLUMBIA ON THE LAUNCHPAD

USA
United States

launch, the ship was still fully protected against the terrible heat. And now that Columbia was in Earth's atmosphere its wings and rudder could work like an airplane's. The pilot, astronaut John Young, began to maneuver it like a glider, swinging it in **S**-shaped curves to make it lose speed and altitude as it came in to land.

This was a turning point in the conquest of space, because before Columbia, every spacecraft returning to Earth had to *fall* through the atmosphere, hanging from huge parachutes, and its reentry had to be carefully calculated. Columbia, controlled by a pilot, could be landed anywhere there was a stretch of ground long enough to allow it to roll to a stop.

Columbia's success convinced most people that this was the spacecraft of the future. It was called a space shuttle because it could move back and forth from Earth to space and space to Earth, just as a shuttle bus travels back and forth between two places. Plans were made to build three more shuttles for the U.S. space program.

Columbia's next three launches, like the first, were mainly tests to make sure the shuttle performed well. Then, in November of 1982, Columbia began to do what it had been intended for. It carried up two small communications satellites in its cargo hold, and they were put into orbit right in space. This was much cheaper and more efficient than if each satellite had been launched separately.

On April 4, 1983, the second space shuttle, named Challenger, was launched. It, too, carried up a satellite to be put into orbit. In June of that year it went up again, and one of its crew was the first American woman to go into space, Dr. Sally K. Ride. Challenger went up once more, in September, and for its return it made the first night landing by a shuttle. In 1984, Challenger was the ship from which two astronauts—U.S. Navy Captain Bruce McCandless and U.S. Army Lieutenant Colonel Robert Stewart—tested rocket propulsion units strapped to their backs, which literally turned them into human spacecraft.

The third shuttle, Discovery, was launched in August, 1984, and in October of 1985, the fourth shuttle, Atlantis, went up for the first time, on a secret mission from the U.S. Department of Defense. Also in October, Challenger was launched on a special mission that was under the control of the European space agency. In its cargo hold, Challenger carried a European-built space laboratory in which a number of experiments with metals, crystals, plant growth, and human reactions to space were carried out. The crew consisted of five American astronauts, two West German scientists, and a Dutch scientist.

Altogether there were 22 shuttle launchings from the first one in 1981 to the end of 1985. They did not all go smoothly. There were numerous times when machinery did not work properly, and there were times when launchings had to be delayed, and even postponed for several days. However, when the launchings were

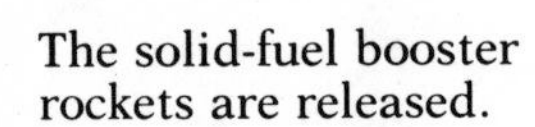

The solid-fuel booster rockets are released.

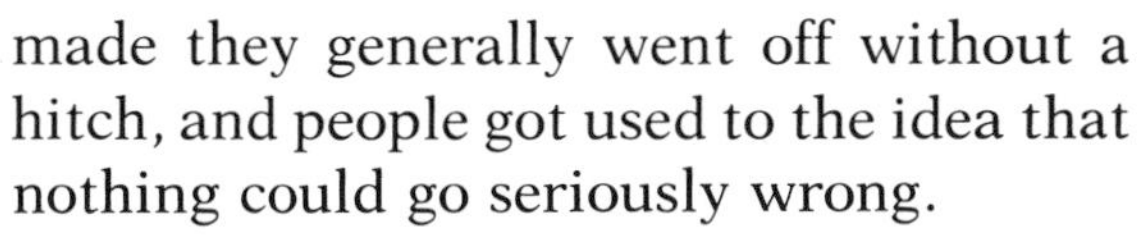

Columbia—Missing Several Protective Tiles

made they generally went off without a hitch, and people got used to the idea that nothing could go seriously wrong.

And then, disaster struck. On January 28, 1986, as the shuttle Challenger rose off the launch pad, carrying a crew of five men and two women, it exploded into a giant fireball. The shuttle was destroyed and everyone aboard it was killed.

This was the worst disaster in the history of the U.S. space program, and the worst catastrophe in the history of spaceflight. Throughout the world, and especially in the United States, there was shock and sadness. The many years of steady success of both the American and Soviet space programs had fooled people into believing that space was completely conquered and that spaceflight had practically become routine. Everyone now realized this was not true.

An investigation into the accident showed that the explosion had been caused by a leak in a joint of one of the booster rockets. The leak had been caused by a rubber ring that did not seal the joint properly because it was stiff from cold weather. It was obvious that the way the booster rockets were put together would have to be completely changed in order to prevent another such tragic accident. The investigation also showed that there were a number of other problems in the construction and engineering of the space shuttles that might cause trouble in the future if not corrected. Therefore, all shuttle flights were halted until all these problems could be taken care of.

In spite of the dreadful Challenger disaster, most spaceflight experts still think space shuttles are the best kind of spacecraft. The U.S. intends to build a new shuttle to replace Challenger; the Soviet Union is apparently building a type of shuttle that will be ready for launching in about 1991; the European Space Agency is developing a shuttle to be launched by 1995; and Japan is testing plans for a shuttle it hopes to have ready by 1999.

However, there are certain to be changes in the way future shuttles will operate. The United States and several other nations are working out plans for a shuttle that will be able to take off like an airplane rather than a rocket, using jet engines powerful enough to carry it into space. Such a craft may well be the manned spaceship of the future.

Repairing a Satellite

Mining an Asteroid

What Lies Ahead?

IN THE STAR-SPANGLED blackness of space 22,300 miles from Earth, a gigantic weblike structure of aluminum girders is being assembled. The tiny, space-suited figures of workers float here and there, bringing beam-ends together, carrying materials from place to place, welding, fastening, tightening. A construction project in space!

Some 10 million miles from Earth, a 2-mile-wide chunk of rock—an asteroid—is speeding on its orbit around the Sun. Close above it hangs a spaceship, while upon its rough surface sits a machine, busily drilling into the rock. A mining operation in space!

Construction projects in space, mining operations in space, power plants in space, even artificial worlds in space—some of these things, and others, will probably come about during your lifetime.

By the end of the 1980's there will probably be one or more permanent space stations in orbit around Earth. These will be structures in which numbers of scientists and technicians live for months at a time, doing work, making observations, and performing experiments that can't be done on Earth. Small space stations such as the U.S. Skylab and the Soviet Salyut, vessels operated by a few people, were put into orbit in the 1970's, but a space station of the future will be larger and probably permanent. It will be a combination astronomical observatory for studying space; laboratory for conducting chemical and biological tests and experiments; test factory for producing things that can't be made on Earth; and missile-launching platform, with comfortable living quarters and a recreation area for the people living in it. The space station will be largely built *in* space, with workers and materials carried into the construction orbit by ships such as the space shuttle Columbia.

Since 1958, scores of artificial satellites performing different kinds of jobs have been sent into orbit. Scientific satellites containing many kinds of instruments provided information about space and things in it. Weather satellites, with instruments for photographing, measuring, and detecting various conditions in Earth's atmosphere, send weather information down to Earth. Communications satellites strengthen radio beams from

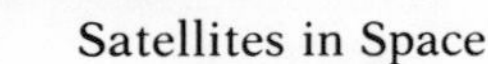

Earth and shoot them back to other parts of the world. In the very near future, improved versions of such satellites, doing better, more complicated jobs, will be carried into orbit by shuttles or will be built right in orbit. One will be a giant orbiting telescope that will be able to find and send information about things that can't even be seen from Earth. Another will be a telecommunication device able to handle hundreds of thousands of phone calls at a time, as well as enable people to tune in TV stations from every part of the world. There are also going to be a good many military satellites in space—devices to spy on other nations and devices to track down and destroy spy satellites. The United States plans to put into orbit a number of devices to destroy any missiles that might be launched against it by an enemy nation—the so-called star wars defense system.

Special purpose spacecraft, like those launched to study Halley's Comet in 1986, will continue to be sent into space in the years to come. A number of planetary probes, to Jupiter, Venus, and Mars, are planned for the future. And by the year 2000, it is probable that people will land on the planet Mars and explore it—most likely Russians or Americans, or Americans and Russians together. In time, there may even be colonies on Mars.

Within the next 25 years, some nations may put power plants into space. Built in orbit, these will be huge devices that can soak up the bright sunlight that fills our area of space, convert it into electricity, and shoot the electricity down to Earth as a microwave beam. On Earth, huge antennas will turn the beam back into electricity for powering large areas. Such electricity from space would be much cheaper than electricity produced on Earth, and having power plants in space would cut down on a lot of Earth's pollution.

Probably within the next 20 to 30 years, machines from Earth will be digging ores out of the surface of the Moon, for Moon rocks contain aluminum, iron, titanium, and some other useful minerals. People and machines will be launched to the Moon, probably from space stations orbiting the Earth. The first people to arrive will have to set up some kind of living quarters on the Moon, and these will probably be made from parts of the very rockets that bring them. A small nuclear power plant will be used to produce oxygen, light, and heat. In time, the living quarters can be made roomier and more comfortable. Perhaps, however, all the work will be done by robots.

Mineral sources even richer than the Moon are the asteroids: the thousands, and perhaps millions, of chunks of rock in orbit between the planets Mars and Jupiter. Probably within 50 to 100 years, people and machines will be visiting some of the larger asteroids to wrest mineral riches from them.

For most people living and working in space stations, on the Moon, and on asteroids, Earth will always be home. Most of them will want to return to it for long vacations at times and will come back to live on Earth when their work is finished or when they retire. But there are probably going to be some people who will make the Moon, an asteroid, or even space itself their home and who will never return to Earth once they leave it. There are going to be children born in space, for whom the Earth will be only a faraway place they may never see! Some of these people will live in communities that grow up around the mines and research centers on the Moon and larger asteroids. Others may live in true space colonies—artificial worlds moving in orbit between the Moon and Earth.

These artificial worlds won't be round balls with people living on the outside of them, like Earth. The kind of artificial world most scientists think would work best would have the shape of a huge ring, about a mile wide, with six spokes leading to a hub in the center, like a wheel. The ring and spokes would be hollow. The inside of the ring would be a space about 400 feet wide, and each spoke would be a corridor about 50 feet wide. The hub would be a round, hollow ball, 400 feet wide. The colony's homes and farming areas would be inside the hollow ring, while the hub would contain an air lock and dock for supply spaceships, machinery, factories, and a recreation area. Some 10,000 people could live in such a wheel in space. It would, however, cost an *enormous* amount of money to put such a colony into space.

Such things as space stations, orbiting power plants, asteroid mining, and even artificial worlds in space are things most scientists think can be done within the next 100 years. But there may well be other major space events that we cannot even dream of now. There may be expeditions to stars. There may be incredible and awesome engineering projects in space and on other planets. The life of the future lies in space, and that life may be so different from what we have now that we can scarcely imagine it!

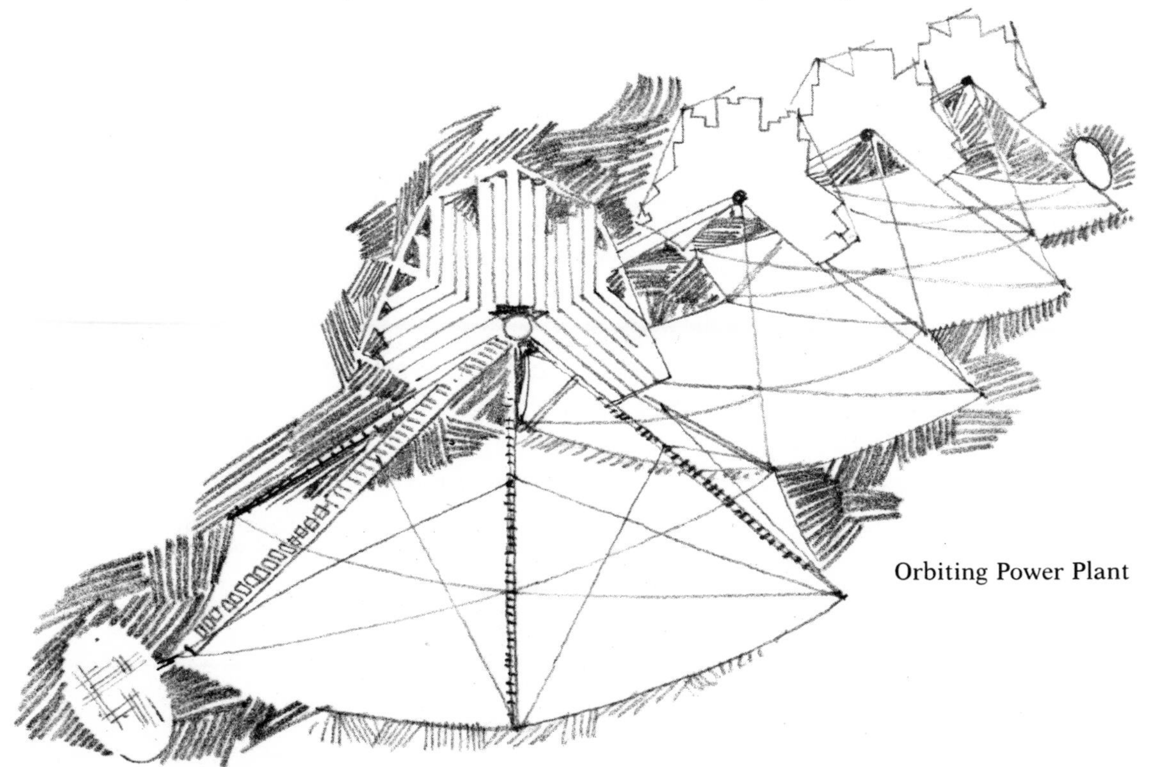

Orbiting Power Plant

Spaceflight Highlights

SPACECRAFT	LAUNCH DATE	CREW	HIGHLIGHTS
Sputnik (USSR)	October 4, 1957	Unmanned	1st spacecraft to orbit Earth
Vostok 1 (USSR)	April 12, 1961	Yuri Gagarin	1st man in space
Mercury 3 (US)	May 5, 1961	Alan Shepard	1st American in space
Vostok 2 (USSR)	August 6, 1961	Gherman Titov	1st day in space (1 day, 1 hour, 18 minutes)
Mercury 6 (US)	February 20, 1962	John Glenn	1st American in orbit
Vostok 6 (USSR)	June 16, 1963	Valentina Tereshkova	1st woman in space
Voskhod 2 (USSR)	March 18, 1965	Pavel Balyayev, Alexei Leonov	1st space walk (10 minutes by Leonov)
Gemini 3 (US)	March 23, 1965	Virgil Grissom, John Young	1st US 2-man space mission
Gemini 4 (US)	June 3, 1965	James McDivitt, Edward White	1st US space walk (21 minutes by White)
Gemini 6 (US)	December 15, 1965	Walter Schirra, Thomas Stafford	Rendezvous to within about 1 foot of Gemini 7
Gemini 8 (US)	March 16, 1966	Neil Armstrong, David Scott	1st docking in space (with unmanned Gemini Agena Target Vehicle); emergency splashdown
Apollo 7 (US)	October 11, 1968	Walter Schirra, Don Eisele, Walter Cunningham	1st manned Apollo flight
Apollo 8 (US)	December 21, 1968	Frank Borman, James Lovell, William Anders	1st manned flight around Moon
Apollo 11 (US)	July 16, 1969	Michael Collins, Neil Armstrong, Edward Aldrin	1st men on Moon—Armstrong and Aldrin land in "Eagle" LM and collect lunar samples
Salyut 1 (USSR)	April 19, 1971	Orbital Space Station	Destroyed October 11, 1971, after about 2,800 orbits
Soyuz 11 (USSR)	June 6, 1971	Georgi Dobrovolsky, Vladislav Volkov, Viktor Patsayev	Docking with Salyut 1; crew later killed during return to Earth
Skylab 1 (US)	May 14, 1973	Unmanned	Damage during lift-off
Skylab 2/Apollo docking craft (US)	May 25, 1973	Charles Conrad, Joseph Kerwin, Paul Weitz	Skylab damaged repaired; exceeded Soviet record of days in space (28 days)
Soyuz 32/Salyut 6 (USSR)	February 25, 1979	Vladimir Lyakhov Valery Ryumin	Crew remains in space a record 175 days. Returns to Earth aboard Soyuz 34
Columbia (US) *STS–1	April 12, 1981	Robert Crippen, John Young	1st space shuttle mission; several heat-resistant tiles lost
Columbia (US) STS–2	November 12, 1981	Joe Engle, Richard Truly	Remote-control "robot arm" tested. Mission cut short due to electrical problems
Challenger (US) STS–6	April 4, 1983	Karol Bobko, Paul Weitz, F. Story Musgrave, Donald Peterson	1st flight of space shuttle Challenger; communications satellite launched; 1st US spacewalk in 9 years
Challenger (US) STS–7	June 18, 1983	Robert Crippen, Fredrick Hauck, John Fabian, Norm Thagard, Sally Ride	1st US woman in space; 1st 5-person shuttle crew; 1st practical use of robot arm (2 satellites launched)
Challenger (US) STS–10	February 3, 1984	Vance Brand, Bruce McCandless, Robert Stewart, Ronald McNair	1st free floating space walk (without a lifeline), using a manned maneuvering unit (MMU)—a kind of jet pack
Challenger (US) STS–11	April 6, 1984	Robert Crippen, Francis Scobee, Terry Hart, James van Hoften, George Nelson	1st satellite repaired in orbit; Long Duration Exposure Facility launched, holding shrimp eggs, seeds, plastics—to see how these fare in space
International Cometary Explorer	September 11, 1985 (flyby)	Unmanned	1st spacecraft to make a flyby of a comet, coming within 4,850 miles of the nucleus of comet Giacobini-Zinner
Challenger (US)	January 28, 1986	Francis Scobee; Michael Smith; Ronald McNair; Ellison Onizuka; Judith Resnick; Gregory Jarvis; Christa McAuliffe	Destroyed during lift-off, causing death of entire crew

*Space Transportation System

Index

Italic page numbers (for example: *8–9, 53*) indicate color illustrations.

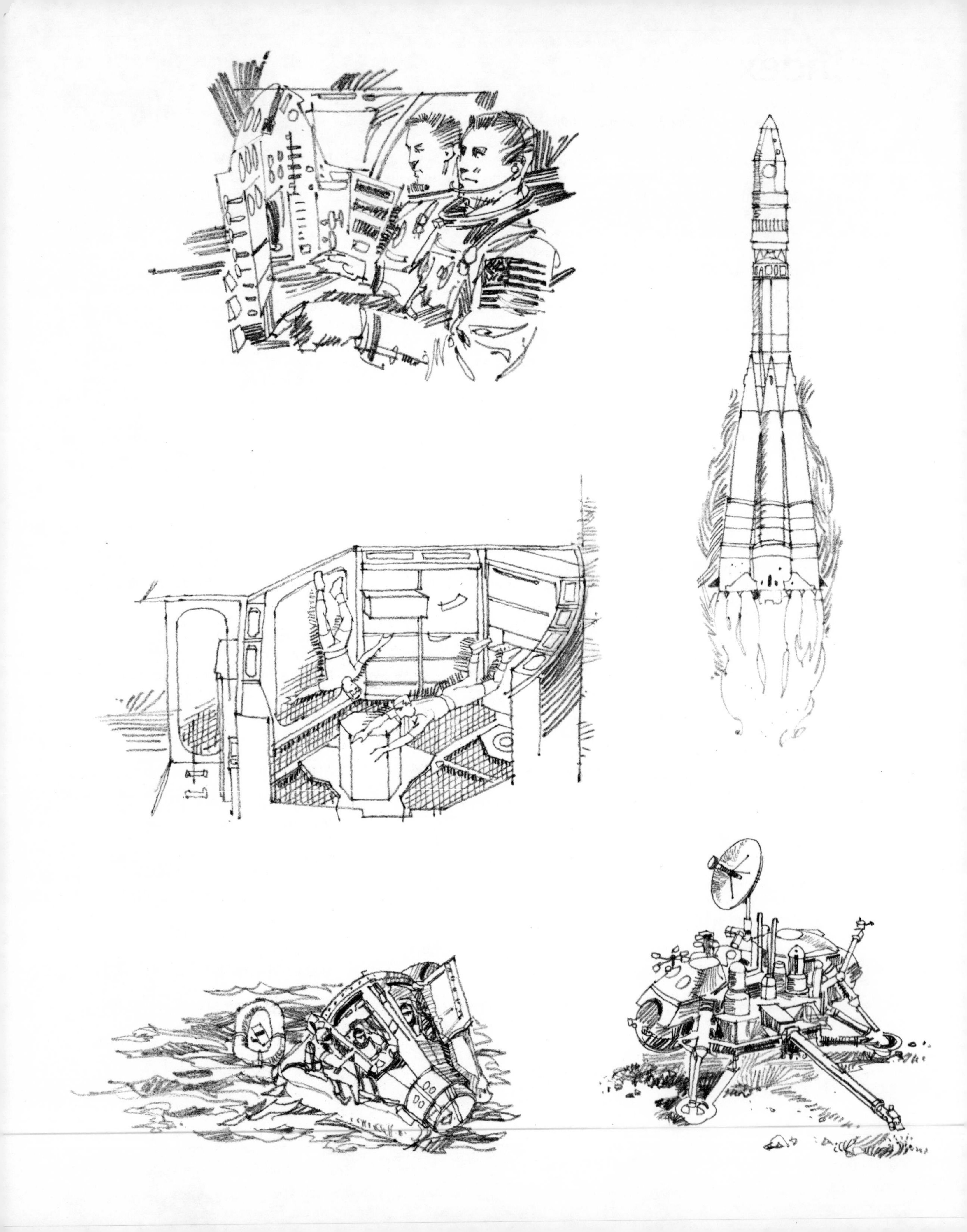

ABCDEFGHIJK